'Brings memories of freedom, and offers a humane view of the past in Indian Country.'

Leonard Peltier, political prisoner, activist and member of the American Indian Movement

'Lest we forget the heart-wrenching resistance of the Sioux and their allies at Standing Rock, Bikem Ekberzade meticulously sets their story in its historic context. This is important, valuable work at a time when Indigenous people all over the world are at the forefront of the struggle for ecological justice.'

Üstün Bilgen-Reinart, author of *Night Spirits: The Story of the Relocation of the Sayisi Dene*

'Shows how the confrontation at Standing Rock fits a centuries-long pattern of oppression, yet also marks the emergence of a growing and increasingly effective Native American resistance to corporate greed and environmental injustice.'

Michael Brune, Executive Director, Sierra Club

'Weaves a much needed and moving story. The book comes alive through the eloquent voices of its Native American organizers, and Ekberzade creates an intimate window into the lives of her subjects. Standing Rock may have its roots in hundreds of years of history but more than ever, this book matters now.'

Donatella Lorch, former foreign correspondent for the *New York Times*

'The story of Standing Rock embodies a long, sad history of violence and broken promises by the US government. Ekberzade carefully documents this history and illuminates it with the words of living Native Americans. An important contribution to our understanding of the US's shameful and often appalling abuse of America's original peoples.'

Nick B. Mills, journalist and author of *Karzai*

About the author

B<small>IKEM</small> E<small>KBERZADE</small> is primarily a photojournalist and documentary photographer, who specialises in forced migration in conflict and post-conflict zones. She has photographed and written two books on refugees, *Illegal* (2006) and *West-end of the Border* (2010), which were part of her documentary photography project The Refugee Project (http://therefugeeproject web.wordpress.com). She has written or contributed to several books and articles, and her photographs have been published by several international newspapers and magazines. Ekberzade is from and is currently based in Turkey.

STANDING ROCK

Greed, Oil and the Lakota's Struggle for Justice

Bikem Ekberzade

ZED

Standing Rock: Greed, Oil and the Lakota's Struggle for Justice was
first published in 2018 by Zed Books Ltd, The Foundry, 17 Oval Way,
London SE11 5RR, UK.

www.zedbooks.net

Copyright © Bikem Ekberzade 2018

The right of Bikem Ekberzade to be identified as the author of this work
has been asserted by her in accordance with the Copyright, Designs
and Patents Act, 1988.

Typeset in Bulmer by T&T Productions Ltd, London
Index by Bikem Ekberzade
Cover design by Steve Marking
Cover photo © Helen H. Richardson/Getty

A catalogue record for this book is available from the British Library

ISBN 978-1-78699-283-3 hb
ISBN 978-1-78699-282-6 pb
ISBN 978-1-78699-284-0 epdf
ISBN 978-1-78699-285-7 epub
ISBN 978-1-78699-286-4 mobi

Contents

Acknowledgements

Without the help of a large number of people, this book would have been a fleeting thought. I would hereby like to thank Julie Mardin, who not only accompanied me on my trip across the Great Plains, but also, when crisis hit, helped me keep things in perspective; Şule Önsel Ekici, with her academic gusto, who was always helping me gain access to archival articles and ample research material in a matter of minutes, and, despite her own workload, without ever turning down any of my overwhelming requests; Natalie Stites, who, despite the massive time difference was always there whenever I needed help locating information, got confused or just needed fresh leads; Marianne Hirsch, who helped me gain unlimited access to the shelves of Columbia University's Butler Library, especially the rare books section; all the people who have spared a considerable amount of their time to tell their stories: LaDonna Tamakawastewin Allard, Douglas White Bull, Julie Garreau, Tammy Joy Granados, Bobbi Jean Three Legs, Foxy Jackson, Will, Chris and Alton; and academics Çağhan Kızıl, Joe Bonni and Alessandra Giannini, for providing me with invaluable information on epigenetics, archaeological surveys and global warming, respectively. I am indebted to them and to all my other friends, who showed their support whenever my confidence in finishing this book ran short. But above all, I owe gratitude to my mother, my only family, who patiently waited for me and on me so I could finish writing this story and file it on time. Also, a big thank-you to those at Zed Books for believing in this book, taking it up on a moment's notice: specifically Ken Barlow, for his editorial suggestions, and Dominic Fagan. Another big thank-you to Ellen White for her meticulous edits, suggestions, revisions and most of all her patience. Finally and most importantly, I would very much like to thank all the authors, researchers and academics out there who are supporting and feeding open access, as I also believe information should be open and free for all.

Prologue

In April 2016, a cry of distress rose from the Standing Rock Sioux Reservation. Perhaps because of the desperation it exhibited, or perhaps as payback for the years of injustice suffered by the Lakota people, this cry found answer in an international response that soon became an expansive avalanche. Despite centuries' worth of breached treaties, continuous forced migration and attempts at assimilation, the Sioux Nation, it seemed, still had one more fight left in them. Soon they would find out that, in this fight at least, they were not alone. People from all over the world, people who felt helpless in the face of large, powerful corporations that were exploiting their much-needed and diminishing resources, rallied to the Lakota people's cause, as did environmentalists, who had been warning the world for decades about the potential disasters awaiting the human race if we did not take care of our planet.

Once people took notice of what was happening at Standing Rock, forgotten human rights abuses and stories of massacres, buried within the thick pages of historical documents written by the colonial masters, started emerging. The Lakota, like most Native Americans, owned an oral tradition: culture, language, history, stories and prophecies had been passed down from generation to generation. Despite the hardships and oppression endured by families stuck in poverty-stricken, suicide-laced reservations, their children and land taken from them, the Lakota way survived. Now, with Standing Rock, the world was once again being reminded of atrocities such as the Wounded Knee and Whitestone massacres as well as numerous other instances throughout the United States' violent history in which tribesmen – despite their open displays of the *wasichu*'s[1] white flag of peace – were slaughtered mercilessly and at times hatefully, while women and children were shot or clubbed to death, their scalps taken by US soldiers as war trophies.

These past cruelties were undertaken for profit, to open up land for settlers so that speculators could reap handsome returns, or to extract precious minerals such as gold from places sacred to tribes, such as the Black Hills. In the present day, meanwhile, to feed Corporate America's insatiable appetite for oil and gas, the Federal Government was once again using physical and psychological coercion against unarmed civilians – this time, including its own citizens.[2] It was also showing the world exactly what it was capable of when confronted with peaceful protest.

Over the course of the United States' colonial history, native tribes were thrown together in what were effectively open-air prisons, with little to no understanding on the oppressors' part of the cultural differences among these peoples. Once confined, attempts by the Federal Government to assimilate them began, and would continue for generations. The process, especially when tribes in the Great Plains were concerned, generally went like this: break tribal unity; erase the role of the tribal chiefs; ban cultural rituals and native languages; and, last but not least, break up families by forcing them to send their children to boarding schools, so that the Indian in them might be killed to "save the man".[3]

This pattern was largely consistent throughout native peoples' encounters with white men: from the early days, when game was plentiful and – through seemingly straightforward trade relations – white traders often ended up taking the lion's share; through to Acts of Congress, land commissions and treaties – when game began to run short – that cannily robbed native tribes of their land. Solving the "Indian Problem" led to attempts at annihilating native societies, culminating in what young people in the reservations now refer to as generational trauma.[4] However, what white men did not manage to erase was the bond that the native people of the Americas share with Mother Earth, a bond so strong it has survived against all the odds.

In the 1930s, an undated manuscript found its way into the annals of the Bureau of American Ethnology: *Indian Tribes of the Upper Missouri*, written by Edwin T. Denig. Upon publication, the magazine's editor announced it safe to attribute the manuscript to the year 1854, due to "internal evidence". These lengthy, detailed notes of Denig provide us with early documentation of the Dakota tribes, including details of life in their camps and the Native Americans' dealings with the ever-growing number of white men that were starting to appear around them. One passage is particularly poignant:

> Before the trade was opened with them by the whites they say they used knives made of the hump rib of the buffalo, hatchets made of flint stone, mallets of the same, cooking utensils of clay and wood, bones for awls, and sinew for thread, all of which articles can yet be found among them. They made with these rude tools their bows and arrows, pointing the latter with stone, and, as game was abundant, hunted them on foot or threw them into pens built for

the purpose, which method they continue to use to this day. In this way they had no difficulty in supporting themselves, and so contend that they have gained nothing by intimacy with the whites but diseases which kill them off in numbers and wants which they are unable at all times to gratify. They have never sold lands by treaty, and the only treaty (with the exception of that at Laramie, 1851) was made by them through an Indian agent of the United States named Wilson, at the Mandan village in 1825. But this was merely an amicable alliance for the protection of American traders and an inducement held out to the Indians to leave off trading at the Hudson Bay Co.'s posts and establish themselves on the Missouri, without, however, any remuneration on the part of the United States.[5]

The symbiotic relationship between the native tribes and their environment was also evident in the names tribesmen chose for their children and for the land they chose to live in or travel through. Native place names were often derived from the geographical or environmental qualities of the areas being referred to, and at times acted as memory markers for prominent events that had taken place there. However, such place names – and thereby the collective memory of a people – would soon be erased by colonial invasion. The settlers replaced indigenous place names with their own references, thus carving their presence into the land. And they didn't stop there. For instance, the Paha Sapa, known by their present-day name the Black Hills, were sacred to the Sioux, who considered them to be the centre of the world. These same mountains would soon bear the faces of four Presidents of the United States. The sacrilege started with digging for gold and continues to this day with attempts at mining uranium in the region, despite objections from tribe members. What remain of the indigenous place names are largely confined to the names of cities and states, referring to the tribes that once roamed those lands: the Iowa, the Omaha, the Mandan.

Epidemics, systematic assimilation, self-serving treaties and mass murder: these are the memories Native Americans have of the white man, the *wasichu*, whom they honoured upon initial contact. In his article "Encounters with spirits",[6] Bruce White tracks down early words used by the Ojibwa and the Dakota in addressing the white traders with whom they dealt. French traders were originally thought of as otherworldly beings due to their skin colour and the curious qualities of the merchandise they were eager to trade with the native population. The tribes honoured the foreigners to the point of reverence in ceremonies during these early encounters: "The Dakota's use of these gestures was also related to their conceptualization of the French as spirits, or as they put it, *wašicun*, a term with several spellings," White notes. Powerful spiritual allies were vital for warrior tribes, so the Dakota "were not interested in just short-term trade; they wanted to establish a long-term relationship in order to obtain French merchandise. They also wanted help in fighting against their enemies." A hasty alliance that would turn sour as soon as the true nature of the white men's desires for the Americas became evident.

Nature and spirituality still shape the Sioux world in the Great Plains, and this is one of the main reasons why the construction of a pipeline potentially disrupting their natural environment is devastating for them. Despite all attempts to bury it beneath a hefty colonial narrative, their native way of life, its folklore and its songs, all still exist in detailed documentation in the archives. Most of this we owe to the diligence of mixed-bloods such as Marie L.

McLaughlin, and to the persistent work of documenters such as Frances Densmore and E. T. Denig. Theirs, and several manuscripts from adventurers, traders and missionaries – admittedly white and highly personal perspectives – shed light on early life in the region. In addition, works by linguists, anthropologists and historians such as Vine Deloria Jr., Raymond DeMallie, Jerome A. Greene and Margot Liberty help paint a picture of what happened in these lands after the natives first interacted with white men, while early collected narratives of native eyewitnesses help us understand the Sioux's traditions and the prominent figures among them. In his ambitious Sioux trilogy, George E. Hyde, although cutting the white man some slack for his ways, nevertheless helps us put things into perspective through a chronological run-down of events in the Heartland. And then there are the original owners of the land themselves: Luther Standing Bear, John Stands in Timber, and Black Elk, among others. Despite a prominent oral tradition, their written works and recorded narratives remain to provide us with the native perspective.

What prompted me to follow the events unfolding at Standing Rock was a basic reporter's instinct, coupled with an old curiosity. However, while trying to understand what was truly going on in the Dakotas, I soon found myself digging further and further into the shelves of hundreds of years of colonial history, trying to map a relative chronology of events ending in April 2016, so as to explain how the native tribes, once the sole rulers of the plains, now stood at the mercy of a white energy conglomerate. Thus, my intention in this book is not simply to provide an account of the protests; rather, I wish to show you how Standing Rock is but one episode in a centuries-spanning story of resistance to exploitation and dispossession.

How and why Standing Rock happened raises profound questions about how indigenous peoples and the environment are treated that cannot be confined simply to the events of 2016. Moreover, though the protest camps may now have been closed down, the fallout continues, and a legacy is emerging. The spirit of Standing Rock was sufficient to spur hundreds of thousands of Native Americans into action, and to come together under a joint flag in order to reclaim what is truly theirs. Although the elders chose to extinguish the Seven Council Fires with the closing of the protest camps, almost a year later, in late February, the youth – untraditional in their defiance – refused to back down and lit the All Nations Fire instead. That fire will be burning across the Americas for decades to come.

Before we begin...

In 2015, with the planet experiencing its hottest years back to back in recorded history, then-President of the United States Barack Obama decided to go green.[1] In his State of the Union address, he announced a commitment to cutting carbon emissions across the United States, citing the Pentagon's warning that climate change posed an immediate risk to the country's national security.[2] Obama's declared commitment still fell far short of a full-scale battle for environmental protection. Indeed, he seemed more worried about forced migration triggered by climate change becoming a possible threat to national security. He did, however, mention that his administration had set aside "more public lands and waters than any administration in history".[3]

With little in his speech denoting a firm commitment to action against climate change, Obama's words nevertheless provided a glimmer of hope for activists, especially those fighting to reduce greenhouse gas emissions. The widely accepted view among environmentalists was that the most effective way to reduce emissions was to keep fossil fuels in the ground. A new buzzword – "dirty fuels" – was being used to describe fossil fuels, the mining and consumption of which placed a heavy burden on the environment, contributing to pollution and, through a high rate of carbon emissions, global warming. So, public lands and waters being "set aside" was a promising start.

The White House's unexpected green agenda was soon reflected in its energy policies. In late 2015, the Obama administration rejected the final phase of a major pipeline project, Keystone XL. President Obama himself stood in front of the cameras to announce he didn't believe the pipeline would make a "meaningful, long-term contribution" to the US economy, and that "shipping dirtier crude oil into our country would not improve America's energy security".[4] He stressed not only that it was vital to keep these "dirty fuels" in the ground to cut emissions, but that, indeed, it was the *only* way.

Obama's rejection of Keystone XL, following years of deliberation and protests, came at a curious juncture for the United States' northern neighbour. A couple of days prior to Obama's declaration, Canada's new prime minister had taken office. A radical change from his conservative predecessor, Justin Trudeau came as a welcome surprise to much of the liberal Left in the world. Trudeau's professed energy policy before becoming prime minister, however, had proved to be a mixed bag. While supporting Keystone XL, he was opposed to the Northern Gateway pipeline, while at the same time getting his party ready to work with the provinces on a cap-and-trade system. This had the environmentalists in the country reeling, and Trudeau was accused of being "all over the map".[5] Adding fuel to the fire, his campaign cochair Dan Gagnier was forced to step down after a memo he wrote to the Canadian energy giant TransCanada became public. Although Gagnier defended his position by saying that the Liberal Party knew of his advisory role to TransCanada, the company building Keystone XL, the contents of the email – detailing how the energy company might deal with a new government in office – were nothing short of scandalous.[6]

So, when on 4 November 2015 Trudeau was sworn into office, the knowledge that the ambitious pipeline project promising to carry oil and gas from the rich sedimentary basin of Hardisty, Alberta to Steele City, Nebraska, and further on to the Gulf of Mexico, would not be realised in effect relieved Canada's new prime minister of a long-term headache.

Keystone XL, if built, would be a repetition of its predecessor, with a shorter and more direct route and a larger carrying capacity than the older Keystone pipeline. Despite being a blow to Canada's already struggling energy sector, Trudeau chose not to make a big thing out of Obama's rejection of the pipeline project. Instead, he shifted his focus to a more popular subject: forced migration. Canada was once again getting ready to welcome refugees.

Obama, in his press conference announcing the cancelation of Keystone XL, declared that he called his counterpart prior to announcing the controversial project's unilateral rejection. Both parties professed that there were no hard feelings. Whether it would have been as painless for the United States to issue this rejection with Trudeau's predecessor Stephen Harper in office, we will never know. But Harper, since the beginning of the project, had placed it at the core of United States–Canada relations, prompting Obama to address in his speech the inflated politicisation of this issue.

The media read Obama's rejection of Keystone XL as the United States gearing itself up for the upcoming climate conference in Paris, with the president determined to position himself as "a champion for the environment"[7] for his last term in office. The Paris talks would begin amidst falling oil prices, meaning the pricey extraction of fossil fuels was no longer a pressing necessity, and end in an ambitious agreement, whereby measures would be undertaken to limit global temperature rises to two degrees Celsius above pre-industrial limits.

During his next State of the Union address in January 2016, a more resolute Obama seemed keen to fly the flag of climate change, as much as an active politician could.[8] His points were clearer, and the part of his speech dedicated to the environment, specifically climate change, was longer. He talked about preserving oil and coal reserves, investing in clean energy and the necessity of traveling to American states that were dependent on fossil fuels for job creation and revenue, to convince them of the new trends in energy. In spite of those seeking to sustain the status quo with respect to the way energy was produced and consumed, he stressed the necessity of a major shift in thinking in order to carry the United States forward. His new stance towards reshaping America's energy policy by furthering investment in clean energy was hailed by climate activists and scorned by large energy conglomerates.

It was in this context that the events unfolding in an otherwise remote area of the United States started going viral. Obama's rejection of the Keystone pipeline had acted as a glimmer of hope for a community trying to preserve their way of life despite relentless negative intrusions from the Federal Government. Since April 2016, there had been a constant flow of people to an otherwise insignificant reservation stuck between the Dakotas, and regardless of the mainstream media's initial resistance to cover the protests, news of the importance of the events unfolding was now filtering out to the rest of the world. The native activists who had protested against Keystone XL were also giving support, hauling their tipis over to the site of their next fight.

When the first camp was set up at the Standing Rock Sioux Reservation to protest against the Dakota Access Pipeline (DAPL), the resistance was portrayed by the mainstream media as a series of minor skirmishes between locals and law enforcement that would soon die away. However, as events unfolded, the camp rapidly grew in size, with new camps popping up in close proximity. The reservation and its surrounding area would soon host thousands of people, including a mix of native tribes from across the Americas, climate activists and non-native civilians, who had all showed up in solidarity. By June 2016, it was no longer possible to ignore what was happening there.

As the world slowly shifted its focus to Standing Rock, the United States was going through an unprecedented presidential campaign, meaning it would be some time before the American mainstream media was truly able to acknowledge what was going down in the Dakotas.

The race for the White House was unusual indeed. Corporate America was running for presidency, and little stood in its way. The Democratic (and indeed Republican) nominees found themselves in uncharted waters as Donald Trump took political debate to radical new lows, maximising on racism and sexism along the way. He did not shy away from showcasing himself as a conscienceless tycoon, and with his followers digging their trenches deep, former Secretary of State Hillary Clinton was forced to concede defeat to a man of little political experience. The campaign left Democrats devastated and the country dangerously polarised. The battle between the two factions had turned into a fight between conventional politics and populism. Populism won.

With Trump's victory assured, the mainstream media turned its attention back to Standing Rock. Obama was still in office, but time was running out to reverse the clock on Dakota Access. Meanwhile, the planet was experiencing its hottest year on record, with eight consecutive months from January to September – with the exception of June – having unprecedented rising temperatures.[9] Climate activists and the native population of the Sioux reservation had to immediately put all possible pressure on Obama, who, they hoped, would in turn put pressure on the US Army Corps of Engineers (USACE) to re-evaluate, reroute or even cancel the project.

Donald Trump was known to be a supporter of old energy policies and a direct investor in energy projects. In his 2015 financial disclosure to the Federal Election Committee, two lines were of particular interest. Trump had invested heavily in Energy Transfer Partners – the company undertaking the construction and later operation of DAPL– and a smaller amount in Phillips 66 – a spin-off[10] of ConocoPhillips, another one of Trump's sizable investments – which would have a 25% stake in DAPL once completed.[11] This made him a direct investor and a major stockholder in the project. A year later, however, the disclosure submitted to the Committee would show Trump's investment in Energy Transfer Partners radically reduced.[12] Still, the organic relationship between Trump and DAPL worked both ways. Energy Transfer Partners' Chief Executive Officer Kelcy Warren had invested heavily in Trump's campaign, with his most recent donation made in June 2016.[13] So, even if Dakota Access was not granted passage by the USACE,[14] there was still the threat that Trump could revoke that decision soon after assuming presidency. By December 2016, he could already be heard declaring to the media that, under his presidency, DAPL would get a green light. On 25 January 2017, exactly four days after he was sworn into office, it did.

Once in the White House, President Trump embarked on an executive order signing spree, reversing the Obama administration's rulings against Keystone XL and DAPL. This act was expected, but what was not predicted was the gagging orders issued to government workers, including scientists working on data related to climate change. The Environmental Protection Agency (EPA) was warned not to post any communique or new data on its website, and government scientists were barred from issuing any press statements or talking to the public about the research in which they were involved. This provoked an immediate public reaction, since it was taxpayer's money that funded the researchers in question. However, there was a greater underlying concern. What if this censorship would soon be followed up by the United States retracting its promises to curb emissions?

While Trump was busy issuing his controversial executive orders, Justin Trudeau was sweating in front of a hostile audience in Calgary, Alberta, trying to explain why extracting fossil fuels from the tar sands was not sustainable. In a video from this question-and-answer session, which went live on his Facebook page the same day, Trudeau could be seen taking a question from a man in the crowd wearing a t-shirt that read "I love oil sands". The man angrily accused Trudeau of rejecting pipeline projects that affected his home province – thereby denying people employment in the pipeline sector – while approving projects elsewhere in Canada. The crowd backed him with loud applause. Trudeau's answer was a detailed explanation of the reasons behind his actions: the necessary transition his country faced from fossil fuels to green energy, and the need for sustainability with regard to Canada's underground resources. He stressed that the excess emissions caused by extracting oil from tar sands were too big a price to pay, before adding:

[Y]ou cannot separate what is good for the environment and what is good for the economy. Do you know who tried to force a choice between the environment and the economy? The last government. They said, we are not gonna do anything on the environment and we are gonna get all these pipelines approved. You know what they did? They didn't get any pipelines approved. Do you know why? Because people didn't have the confidence that they were building for the long-term, that they were creating the jobs and the opportunity of the future, because they refused to accept the fact that the way to build a strong economy for the future is to protect the environment at the same time.[15]

Such sentiments were nowhere in evidence in the Trump White House. With the president in office only a couple of weeks, things had already started heating up in North Dakota. Following the executive orders to fast track the two controversial pipelines, on 7 February 2017 the USACE retracted its decision not to grant easement, or right of passage, to Energy Transfer Partners, allowing them to build underneath Lake Oahe and, by extension, across the Missouri River. With easement granted and the official two-week waiting period hastily waived, construction on the pipeline resumed. Following this, USACE issued a flood warning, asking that all protest camps be evacuated by 22 February.

With a forbidding climate intensified by the subzero temperatures of the Dakota winter, living conditions in the camps were difficult already. The majority of protesters left following the army's directive to empty the camps, but a small number stayed behind, determined to hold their ground. By the end of February, all camps, including those within the borders of Standing Rock Sioux Reservation, were forcibly shut down. The only alternative left for the Sioux Nation was to continue their fight in federal courts. Once again, the United States Federal Government was trying to lower a shroud of silence over the Sioux Reservation by shifting the battlefield away from media attention: the long and tedious courtroom hearings would slowly but surely extinguish all interest, they hoped. However, they made one crucial miscalculation: the impact of social media. Just as the effects of the story on the headlines of major news outlets dimmed, the internet lit up with messages of support and determination as well as a steady stream of communication on developments regarding DAPL and Standing Rock.

Meanwhile, the Trump administration's environmental policy was becoming crystal clear. On 2 June 2017, Trump himself announced his decision to pull out of the Paris Agreement. "In order to fulfil my solemn duty to protect America and its citizens, the United States will withdraw from the Paris Climate Accord," he declared, adding that his government would "begin negotiations to re-enter" on terms more amicable to the United States. The European Union (EU) lost no time in declaring there would be "no re-negotiation of terms". British newspaper *The Guardian* reported European officials' decision to deal with the United States on all matters pertaining to the implementation of the Paris Accord at state rather than federal level with the headline: "EU to bypass Trump administration after Paris climate agreement pull-out".[16]

A couple of weeks later, on 14 June, the Standing Rock Sioux Tribe won a small victory. A federal judge, in response to the tribe's objection to the USACE granting easement to Energy Transfer Partners, ruled that "the U.S. Army Corps of Engineers failed to perform an adequate study of the pipeline's environmental consequences when it first approved its construction". Though the decision did not halt construction, it explicitly stated that the USACE "did not adequately consider the impacts of an oil spill on fishing rights, hunting rights, or environmental justice, or the degree to which the pipeline's effects [were] likely to be highly controversial."[17]

The events surrounding Dakota Access and the resistance at Standing Rock may appear to be a series of environmental protests, with the energy sector and big money pitted against climate activists. However, although these events are directly linked to the proposed construction of a pipeline, there is far more to it than that. The Lakota people of the Great Sioux Nation have a long and proud history of standing up to human rights abuses, and an equally traumatic one of slaughter and assimilation en masse. Notwithstanding countless disappointments at the hands of the Federal Government, massacres by the army and unjust imprisonments, and despite many of their people becoming entrapped in a cycle of poverty, petty crime, unemployment, and alcohol and drug abuse, the Lakota's bond with the land and the creatures that live above and below it has never ceased. So, when they felt that their land was being threatened, the Sioux gave out a cry: one that continues to resonate today, long after the camps have been dismantled.

The chapters ahead attempt to detail the complicated roots of the resistance at Standing Rock: its beginnings, the story of the Lakota people and their historical dealings with the Federal Government, reservation blues and how not much has changed on the continent since the *wasichu* first set foot on it.

That said, the story of Standing Rock comes at a curious time for our planet. With climate refugees now a reality rather than mere theory, and pollution threatening the livelihoods of people across the globe, this is also the story of how we as human beings need to decide how to move forward with our lives.

ONE | The resistance

Upon suffering beyond suffering; the Red Nation shall rise again and it shall be a blessing for a sick world. A world filled with broken promises, selfishness and separations. A world longing for light again. I see a time of seven generations when all the colours of mankind will gather under the sacred Tree of Life and the whole Earth will become one circle again. In that day there will be those among the Lakota who will carry knowledge and understanding of unity among all living things, and the young white ones will come to those of my people and ask for this wisdom. I salute the light within your eyes where the whole universe dwells. For when you are at that center within you and I am that place within me, we shall be as one.
(Prophecy of Oglala Chief Crazy Horse)

At the Prairie Knights Casino

"So. My name is LaDonna Bravebull Allard. My real name is Tamakawastewin, Her Good Earth Woman. I am an enrolled member of Standing Rock Sioux Tribe. I am Ihunktonwan Pabaksa and Sisseton Dakota on my father's side. I am Hunkpapa, *Sihasapa* and Oglala Lakota on my mother's side. So, my father is Frank Bravebull, whose father was John Bravebull, whose father was Claudius Bravebull, whose father was Si-tanka Ohitika, whose father is Aspula. On my father's side. Let's see;

there is my father, his mother Agnes, and Agnes' mother was Holy Generation Woman, who is married to Tatanka Ohitika. Holy Generation's mother was Pretty Door, and her father was Wind on His Forehead. And on my mother's side there is my mother, Valerie Lovejoy. My grandmother Alice's mother was Agnes Dog: Agnes Dog's father was Dog, and her mother was Pte Ska Win, White Buffalo Woman, and she was the daughter of Red Thunder, and Red Thunder was the son of Bear Face, and Bear Face was the son of Iron Horn, who was son of Makoche. Red Thunder had six brothers: Iron Horn, Shaved Head, Bear Face, Little Bear and Rain in the Face. And all these are my relatives."

We were gathered around a small table inside the restaurant section of the Prairie Knights Casino, some 16 miles north of Fort Yates in Standing Rock Sioux Reservation. LaDonna, greeting the locals filtering in as she sat proudly upright, facing the entrance to the dining hall, continued to recite her long lineage as per my request without flinching. Beyond us in the main hall the mostly empty gambling area was lit by the colourful lights of the slot machines. Behind our table stood the extensive open buffet, and although it was well past lunch time, people were still moving in and out of the place with their plates full.

It had been difficult securing an interview with her. Following several emails, Facebook messages, phone calls, texts, and me reminding her of the dates I would be in North Dakota through every medium afforded by technology, here we finally were: LaDonna, a graceful woman with big, beautiful eyes that silently spoke of times past; her adorable grandson, Joshua; myself; and another journalist, who was writing for a Polish newspaper and had already started with her questions by the time I got there.

After she was done listing her ancestors' names, a process during which we all held our breaths (apart for Joshua, who continued silently playing a game on his tablet), I asked LaDonna whether it was true that Rain in the Face got his name because his mother left him briefly outside their tipi during a rain shower. "Nah," she replied, "that's all in the internet." I mumbled that I actually saw it in an old book I had discovered at Columbia University's Butler Library. Looking at me directly, she explained that, in their culture, a person could have up to four names during their lifetime. These consisted of a baby name; a kid name; an adult name, which you had to do a feat to earn; and finally, "when you are an elder, you can give your name to somebody below you and then you take another name". "My name came from a dream," she went on, laughing briefly before continuing: "The man who gave me the dream said that he had seen me standing on the earth, barefooted, with a cup of water in one hand and bread in the other, and I was welcoming people. And so they named me Her Good Earth Woman. Because he said, 'one day, you are gonna welcome people.' So. Names come in very different ways, and names change, in many different ways. And so there is no one way." After a short pause, she reflected: "even Rain in the Face took his name after he was an adult." Then, thinking over my question, she added: "but I read that on the internet once. I think when people seem to ask us things, they assume things. And so they write them down."

Gran'ma posts on YouTube

For the Sioux, as with many Native American Tribes, their women have a special place. They are held in high esteem, bordering on reverence, and are taught to fight at an early age, so they can

defend themselves; to rule as tribal chiefs when it becomes necessary; and to carry the sacred medicine bundle. They are important members of society, where their wisdom is often adhered
to as they become elders. Perhaps because of this, Native North
American women often have a relaxed, self-confident air about
them, and are easy to engage while being slightly intimidating.

LaDonna Bravebull Allard is no exception. It was unsurprising
that she did what she did on the morning of 13 July 2016, when she
received the news that heavy machinery was getting ready to disturb the earth around her reservation: "I was in Albuquerque at a
meeting, and I said, wow, now what do we do? So I just went to my
room, picked up my cellphone, and begged people come help me."

And they did, responding to the desperate call LaDonna
recorded on her mobile phone and posted on the internet:
first in small groups, but at a steady flow, meaning the camp-
grounds would soon have to be expanded to house hundreds
of people. Not long afterwards, thousands more would arrive
and stay. LaDonna recalls a friend asking her how many people
she thought would show up after she posted her video on You-
Tube. She says she responded that even fifty people showing
up would make her happy. Later, when she came over the hill
and saw how many were there: "I just had to pull off [sic] the
car and cry because I couldn't believe it." Still, the people kept
coming. One person that sticks in her mind is a sixty-four-year-
old woman from West Virginia, who in response to the question
"Why did you come here?" replied, "I waited for this call my
whole life." So, when it at long last came from Standing Rock,
the woman told LaDonna that she had sold her home, in fact,
had "sold everything, and put it in this car and come here to
stand with you."

Sitting at the Prairie Knights Casino exactly a year after everything started, LaDonna couldn't help reminiscing how the camp, Sacred Stone, first came to be, and how everything had in fact started months before she posted her video on the internet. "The chairman had set up meetings, went out to the communities, and was telling them about the proposed pipeline, and I was sitting in the meeting down in the foyer, and this lady named Joye Braun, and Jasilyn and this youth said that they were in the XL pipeline fight. Would we be willing to set up a camp?" When no one in the room responded either way, LaDonna decided to take up the offer: "I said, 'I have some land', and they said, 'well, show us', and so I took them out there". By the next day, Jasilyn Charger, Wiyaka Eagleman, Joseph White Eyes and Joye Braun were convinced that LaDonna's plot of land would be their new campground. "They said, 'so, when do you wanna start a camp?' I was like, 'I don't know how', and they said 'OK, we'll do it on April 1'. I said, 'in five days?'. They said 'yes', and so within five days, three tipis went up."

Soon the camp LaDonna allowed to be set up on her property would explode with new arrivals. Many more camps would open up around hers, across the Cannonball River, all the way up to where heavy machinery sat ready to plough the earth, cordoned off by private security and their attack dogs. Things were not always peaceful, as LaDonna would shortly afterwards describe in painful detail for *The Guardian* newspaper:

While we stand in prayer, we have assault rifles aimed at us, we are attacked by dogs, pushed from our sacred sites with pepper spray, shot with rubber bullets and bean bag rounds and Tasers, beaten with sticks, handcuffed and thrown in dog kennels. Our horses have been shot and killed. Our elders have been dragged out of ceremonies, our sacred bundles seized, our sacred eagle staff pulled from our hands. My daughter was stripped naked in jail and left overnight for a traffic violation. An arsonist set the hills across from our camp afire, and for hours Morton County did nothing but prevent tribal authorities from responding.[1]

Despite the threats of violence from private security and state police, people continued to turn up in large numbers, while those already there stood their ground. Until the winter blizzards hit the harsh terrain, the self-proclaimed water protectors stayed in tipis, yurts,[2] tents, caravans and old abandoned buses, praying together for the water and the planet. It was the brutal violence unleashed upon this peaceful form of civil disobedience that convinced many people watching the events unfolding at Standing Rock that something was truly amiss.

These events did not unfold over the course of a month or a year. Before the Standing Rock Sioux Tribe decided to stand up against a white corporation, before LaDonna recorded and posted online her video asking people to come stand with them, there had been centuries' worth of human right abuses, land grabs and resource exploitations that were at least given a green light by the Federal Government, if not directly enacted by them on the native population in the Dakotas. Now, thanks to Standing Rock, these stories began surfacing once more, and subjects such as assimilation, invasion, removal, annihilation and trauma were finally being talked about.

Reframing land

The river junction north of the reservation, which is now flooded and has been turned into a man-made reservoir, was sacred for the Sioux; hence the name of the first camp on reservation soil, Sacred Stone.

"When I was a child," explains LaDonna, "the Cannonball River would hit the Missouri River and there used to be this whirlwind." As kids, she and her brother would climb over the train bridge that used to cross the river and try to hold on to the rafters, which shook with each oncoming train. "I never thought ever we would fall in the river. My grandma would have really gotten after us if she knew." From up there, they could see the whirlwind and that "it made these huge round sand stones". She remembers the river being littered with them. Thus, when the time came to pick a name for the camp, she already had an answer: The Place That Makes The Sacred Stones.

Missouri's Lakota name is Inyan Wakangapi Wakpa, or, as LaDonna tells us, The River that Makes the Sacred Stones. Cannonball River, is a tributary to the Missouri, and together they form the northern and eastern boundaries of the Standing Rock Sioux Reservation, converging at the north-eastern corner. Throughout the colonial era, most Native American place names were replaced by non-native ones. However, thanks to oral history, some native names survive today, despite being wiped off official maps by colonial masters. LaDonna, acting as per her title of Tribal Historian, explains that when the expedition of Lewis and Clark arrived in 1804,[3] "they've seen all these round sandstones, and the only thing they could equate [them] to is cannonballs. And so they named the Cannonball River and the community Cannonball," with complete disregard for any native name that existed prior.

Despite the thousands of miles between them, and given their linguistic and cultural differences, the Apache of Cibecue have a similar approach to that of the Sioux when it comes to naming the land: one where land names act as pointers in their oral history. To exemplify the importance of land and place names in Apache culture, it is worth taking a minute to visit linguistic anthropologist Keith Basso's work on Apache place names and the stories behind them:

> the past is a well-worn "path" or "trail" (*'intin*) which was travelled first by the people's founding ancestors and which subsequent generations of Apaches have travelled ever since. Beyond the memories of living persons, this path is no longer visible – the past has disappeared – and thus it is unavailable for direct consultation and study. For this reason, the past must be constructed – which is to say, imagined.

This is often done with the aid of what the Apaches call "footprints" or "tracks", meaning memorial markers dropped throughout their historical past. Via these markers, the stories survive into the present. As Basso continues to tell us, these markers may take different forms, "including Apache place-names, Apache stories and songs, and different kinds of relics found at locations throughout Apache country". He stresses that "what matters most to Apaches is *where* events occurred, not when, and what they serve to reveal about the development and character of Apache social life".[4] What Basso has discovered about the Western Apache holds true for most native tribes, including those who inhabit the Great Plains.

Assimilation comes in many forms, and attempting to erase the collective memory of an indigenous group by meddling with place names is one. While native names may be inherited by other tribes moving into new territories through warfare or other means, a process as political as colonialism constitutes a different case entirely. Erasing a person's past and trying to situate them in settler society as a lower caste is key to controlling that person. Thus, replacing place names that are familiar to a native tribe with names of soldiers, politicians and even presidents of the new order is one way to consolidate power over the oppressed. As names disappear, stories are lost and history forgotten. Geography loses its markers, and the change in ownership of the land is rendered complete.

BOX 1. The etymological conundrum

The origins of most Native American tribal names familiar to us through the "white" media share a similar fate to native place names: Western explorers and later settlers would name the original inhabitants of areas they were now claiming ownership of as they saw fit.

For example, the name Mohawk in effect refers to an eastern arm of the Haudenosaunee/Iroquois Confederacy, and the tribesmen would much rather be called their original name, Kanien'kehaka. Mohawk is a name derived from an Algonquian reference that carries overtones of cannibalism. The Kanien'kehaka, a name that roughly translates as "people of the flint place", were traders, rumoured to be fierce fighters and natural enemies of the Algonquian tribes. However, the Dutch and later the French used the name Mohawk in reference to this tribe, and the white media, along with a string of Hollywood movies, helped to nail it in place.

Another example is the Comanche, an arm of the Shoshone tribe, who broke off and moved into the Southern Great Plains.

Their chosen name was Nermernuh, but the westerners preferred to refer to them using the derogatory word that the Ute, their enemies, applied to them. In Ute, Comanche means "anyone who wants to fight me all the time".[5]

It should therefore be unsurprising that the case is no different for the Sioux. The name Sioux was first used by the young explorer Jean Nicolet in 1640 and is popularly accepted to be derived from the Ojibwa word *nadouessioux*, meaning "enemies", which the Ojibwa used for their southern neighbours.

As a result of Standing Rock, all of these mistakes, misunderstandings and misnomers are now getting a chance to be corrected. This applies not only to the renaming of tribes: hopefully the misinterpreted struggles and lost histories of these peoples can also find sympathetic ears that are ready to listen and take notice. Through the struggle for survival at Standing Rock, the numerous massacres these lands have witnessed can also, and at last, be justly shared, with the hope that the carnage our planet is currently facing may be averted.

The case for the Black Hills, or the Paha Sapa

Here once the warriors stood in their glory. Mothers played with their infants and gazed on the scene with the warm hopes of the future. The aged and weak sat down but they wept not. They would soon be at rest in the regions where the Great Spirit dwelt, in a home prepared for them beyond these western skies. But this region, the last one they called their home, they could not long call their own. Before the greed of the pale-face and the steel they faded as the snow melts away before the vernal sun.
(Reverend Peter Rosen, from his book *Pa-Ha-Sa-Pah*)[6]

Karl Schlesier, in the introduction he wrote for a compilation of essays on archaeological markers in the Great Plains,[7] argues that ethnicity is something people take with them and adapt to their new surroundings when they migrate. Similarly, religious faith, which is what ethnicity is primarily built upon, is also adapted to these new surroundings. With the complex nature of settlement in the Great Plains in mind, he tells us:

> The territories of ethnic groups often changed over time. In new territories, new ethnic markers were established. Often the sacred places of earlier – even evicted – groups were adopted because they were natural landmarks and powerful, impressive locations. In a sense immigrating groups brought their sacred places with them.[8]

The Black Hills offer one example of this adaptive belief system holding a symbiotic relationship with nature. This area, known to the Lakota as Paha Sapa, is revered as the centre of the world. In the 1930s, legendary Oglala Lakota medicine man Black Elk spoke of a vision he had when he was a boy: "I looked ahead and saw the mountains there with rocks and forests on them, and from the mountains flashed all colours upward to the heavens. Then I was standing on the highest mountain of them all, and round about beneath me was the whole hoop of the world." Where Black Elk stood in his vision is later revealed to us as possibly being Harney (now Black Elk) Peak in the Black Hills.[9]

Archaeologist Linea Sundstrom, having also written about the sacred geography of the Black Hills, explains using specific examples how the Lakota adapted their belief system to this geography.[10] She mentions them identifying "several natural features in the Black Hills with constellations". The Lakota would also associate these constellations with individual stories from their own mythology, and thus "people's seasonal movements and their retelling of the Falling Star myths corresponded with these landscape features".[11]

The Lakota, the final inhabitants of the Black Hills before white men came, were not the only ones who considered these hills sacred: the Cheyennes and the Suhtais, the Arapahoes, and, even earlier, Comanche groups and possibly Kiowas and Kiowa-Apaches, who inhabited the area, also centred their belief systems and creation myths on these impressive hills.[12] In his book *Pa-Ha-Sa-Pah*, penned in 1895, Reverend Peter Rosen theorises that the chronology of the settlement of the Black Hills goes even further back, as far as the Toltecs.[13] He notes that the Mesoamerican people, whose empire is commonly attributed to central Mexico, may in fact have originally inhabited areas further north than thought, such as the Great Plains.[14]

Schlesier points out that the Suhtais (early inhabitants of the Northern Plains), after migrating to the Black Hills around 1670, also transferred their origin story of the *New Life Lodge* ceremony from their sacred mountain in the Timber Mountains of Minnesota to Bear Butte in the Black Hills.[15] For the Lakota, who migrated into the area in the seventeenth century from the Great Lakes, coming out of the endless plains and seeing these hills, thick and dark with timber, must have made quite an impression: enough to make them the centre of their universe.

Thus, ownership of the Black Hills is a highly sensitive and complex topic. The "official" version of history tells us that the Ojibwa and the Cree, armed with new tools of warfare acquired from French traders and looking to advance their trading power, pushed any competition that got in the way to the west and the south, forcing the Lakota to migrate; the Lakota, in turn, came as far as the Black Hills region, choosing to settle in an area where both timber and bison were still plentiful. This account empha-sises that the Lakota migration was a relatively recent affair, with the western Lakota bands arriving in the area in 1775. Leaving out the complex web of indigenous tribes in the area as well as their settlement chronology prior to the Lakota migration and the current number of tribes who still consider the area sacred is a problematic simplification on several accounts, playing down the native claim to the landmass as a sacred dwelling.

This official draft of history can be traced back to the discovery of gold in the Black Hills in 1874. It also coincides with westward expansion and the US government's policy of confining tribes to their respective reservations in order to ensure safe passage for settler communities. To this day, the Lakota maintain that they never signed away the Black Hills in any treaty. However, this has not deterred the US government from digging in this sacred landmass for minerals, harvesting its trees for timber and carving the faces of its presidents on the Six Grandfathers, while chang-ing the mountain's native name to Mount Rushmore.

Basso's reflections on place names again find root here when one considers this renaming of the Six Grandfathers after Charles E. Rushmore. As the story goes, Rushmore, a New York-based busi-nessman and attorney, travelled to the Black Hills to check on land titles for a fellow New York-based businessman, whose interests lay in mining activities in the region. His guide was a local miner. On their daily treks, Rushmore saw the Six Grandfathers, and one day asked his guide what the mountain was called. The guide replied: "Never had any, but it has now – we'll call the thing Rushmore."[16]

The reason for Charles Rushmore's original visit to South Dakota continues to define the fight over the Black Hills today. An area still rich in mineral deposits, it is heavily targeted by corporations, despite opposition from locals, natives and non-natives alike. The plunder in Paha Sapa for the native tribes means sacrilege, whereas for the locals who still live in the area it dictates their survival.

One relatively recent predator is a US subsidiary of a Canadian company, Powertech Uranium Corporation, acquired by Azarga Resources Limited in 2014,[17] which is looking to extract uranium ore in the area south-west of the Black Hills. The proposed technique to be applied at the Dewey Burdock mine is similar to fracking: it involves pumping in large quantities of chemically treated water to dissolve and unearth the mineral. However vigorously the mining company's lobbyists might be promoting the technique as "safe", there is no guarantee that the chemically treated water won't leak into the ground waters. For the residents of the Pine Ridge Reservation, this is something with which they are all too familiar.

In 2015, the non-profit environmental organisation Defenders of the Black Hills conducted tests on the five water wells that provided most of the drinking water to the Pine Ridge Reservation. The tests revealed radioactive contamination in all of them. The finger has been pointed at the uranium mine at Crow Butte, with the Defenders explicitly stating in a newsletter that "the potentiometric surface map of the underground aquifers shows the movement of water from Crow Butte to beneath the Pine Ridge Reservation. The experts from consolidated interveners showed that the aquifers leak into each other."[18] The newsletter went on to state that the uranium isotope ratio proves that the source of the contamination for the Pine Ridge wells is the mine at Crow Butte.

Charmaine White Face, a soft-spoken woman in her seventies, is a former board member and coordinator of the recently retired Defenders. Above all else, though, she is a mother, and while addressing a rally in 2016, these were the words with which she chose to start her speech: "I've already had cancer. My father died from cancer, my daughter has cancer, my son is dying from lupus[19] as I stand here and speak." Charmaine and her Defenders have fought against uranium mining and contamination in the Black Hills area for over fourteen years. When I ask her why they have chosen to stop, she points out that despite being "proud of the awareness we brought on many issues", she is now seventy years old and must care for her son, who has a terminal illness. "I cannot put in the time it takes to run the organization, and no one else wanted to do it."

Though the Defenders may have announced their retirement, that does not mean they are defunct. As Charmaine explains:

> One of our unwritten rules of Defenders is that when a project has many people involved, like the Dewey Burdock project, then we step back and go on with another project. Although Defenders has mostly shut down, we still are a part of a national campaign, which we started, to clean up the 15,000 plus abandoned uranium mines in the United States.

The environmental organisation's fight against Powertech's, and later Azarga's, application to operate the Dewey Burdock mine goes back to 2004. With Charmaine acting as the Defenders' lawyer, they even took the South Dakota Board of Minerals and Environment to court, an act she says "delayed the project for a while". However, the Board retaliated, claiming that "non-profits could not act *pro se* [i.e., on one's own behalf]". Charmaine says that the Board's action was "a civil rights violation to deny us the right to defend ourselves". The Defenders may have lost their case in court, but by then the movement to fight Dewey Burdock had expanded into a consortium that included over 200 other civil initiatives. In 2017, in an unprecedented attempt to convince locals of the safety of in situ leaching (ISL), EPA conducted a number of community hearings between April and May. The irony of EPA trying to convince locals of the procedure's safety, as opposed to requesting that the companies applying for permits submit solid proof of the safety of their techniques, was obvious to everyone concerned. Thus, throughout these outreach meetings, citizens from communities potentially affected by the proposed mine strenuously made clear their desire to not have permits granted to the mining company. Each person who stood up spoke about direct or familial experience of harm hitherto caused by other mines, which were not closely regulated and had previously contaminated the drinking water of nearby towns and reservations alike. The citizens' concerns covered a wide range of topics, from cancer rates to animal deaths in Pine Ridge caused by uranium seeping into the aquifers and ponds. One participant in these community meetings rightfully stated that he was uncertain whether or not their concerns would be heeded. At the time of writing, with permits seemingly on a fast track to being granted, this seems a depressingly remote possibility.[20]

Despite EPA having already issued draft permits in the summer of 2017 to Powertech for operating the Dewey Burdock mine, the events at Standing Rock have united the native tribes and locals, whose lives are directly at risk, under the slogan *mni wiconi*, Lakota for "water is life": the phrase that became central to the movement at Standing Rock. The sacred nature of the Black Hills is also help-ing to get the message across. As LaDonna tells us:

> Each indigenous people takes care of part of the Mother Earth. The heart, the lungs, the arms, the eyes. But we, our nation, is the heart of the world. The Black Hills, when you look at it from the sky, it is shaped like a human heart. Our heart is the Black Hills. Because it is the heart of the world, according to our belief. In South America, Bolivia, the Amazon, and the trees are the lungs of the world. And they help the world breathe. Each of us have an obligation to the world. And I don't think we understand that.

Still, when one takes a look at the transcripts of EPA meetings regarding the Dewey Burdock mine and listens to the concerns of the citizens who attended those meetings, it becomes clear that, post-Standing Rock, we may have finally started to understand after all.

The case for the Oahe Reservoir

Much like the case of the Black Hills, another way to make it dif-ficult, if not impossible, for native owners to reclaim land is by changing the landscape altogether. This is exactly what started happening in the 1940s in the Dakotas. The Missouri River, also known as the "Big Muddy", was infamous for its flood path. Major floods had devastated those living next to it in 1844, 1881, 1903, 1915, 1926 and 1934.

Although back in 1878 the Sioux had not wanted to move to "the sickly low lands near the river" that harboured memories of disease and death, they were eventually left with little choice. Car-rying rations from distribution points along the Missouri River inland was an undertaking the Federal Government was not eager to spend further energy, time or money on. Soon, the Lakota chiefs would have to accept the promise that, once they moved, they would only have to remain there for one year before being allowed to move back to the high country.[21] However, reality would prove far different. The greatest beneficiary of this move was the Federal Government: it was simply cheaper to accommodate the tribesmen in their new locale. The promise that the tribesmen would be allowed to return to higher ground was never revisited by Washington. As far as they were concerned, the move of the Oglala band of Chief Red Cloud and the Brulé band of Chief Spotted Tail was final. As historian George E. Hyde tells it, the tribes:

> could not comprehend that it cost the government over one dollar per hundred pounds per hundred miles to haul rations and other supplies to the old Red Cloud and Spotted Tail agencies in northwestern Nebraska and that Congress wished to save this expense by placing the new agencies on or near the Missouri, where they could be cheaply supplied by water transportation up the river.[22]

And so, because of (1) the Federal Government's policy of spending as little as possible in order to meet their obligations under the 1851 and 1868 Fort Laramie treaties with the tribes, despite these obligations being meagre compensation for the vast lands ceded; (2) land speculators' greed, advertising "vacant" Dakota lands with much gusto to white settlers without properly explaining the harsh climate that accompanied them; (3) the incorrigible Dakota droughts; and (4) the old reservation lands, forcibly taken from tribes and on which white farmers were by now settled, desperately needing irrigation and flood control, more land belonging to the Standing Rock Sioux Tribe would need to be wrested from its true owners to make room for the Oahe Dam and Reservoir.

At such a juncture, the Big Muddy flooded again, three times during the course of 1943. The floods were particularly severe, creating a window of opportunity for the Federal Government to intervene.

Two agencies – one the Bureau of Reclamation (BOR), acting under the Department of Interior, and the other the USACE, acting under the Department of Defense – had separate plans in place to address these floods along the Missouri basin. As a result, in early 1944 USACE's Pick Plan, which included the building of dams to ease navigation along the Missouri and levees to control flooding, was immediately challenged by BOR's Sloan Plan, which proposed building several infrastructure projects along the Missouri to alleviate the irrigation needs of white farmers. The two competing agencies, following much haggling over whose plan was best, were forced to reconcile, and the joint Pick–Sloan Plan was formulated.

Both plans were written primarily with white settlers and farmers in mind. Once again, the native population whose reservations bordered the Missouri were seen as a minor detail to be dealt with, while the joint plan passed in Congress as part of the Flood Control Act. Even so, leaving a large group of civilians out of federal planning concerned some. This sentiment would be voiced several times in the House of Representatives during numerous hearings on the building of the Oahe Dam, a project proposed by the Pick–Sloan Plan.

On Wednesday, 13 July 1949, as the Committee on Public Lands convened at the House of Representatives, a bill was brought forth which proposed that time should be taken to negotiate with tribesmen, rather than rush the decision to relocate families from the construction area and start the project. It was introduced by South Dakota Senator Francis Case and meticulously titled: *A bill to authorize the negotiation, approval, and ratification of separate settlement contracts with the Sioux Indians of Cheyenne River Reservation in South Dakota and of Standing Rock Reservation in South Dakota and North Dakota for Indian lands and rights acquired by the United States for the Oahe Dam and Reservoir, Missouri River development, and for other purposes* (H.R. 5372).

Following the reading of the proposed bill and a few technical remarks, Senator William Lemke voiced his opinion that this bill was unnecessary. He insisted they should hurry the project along, rather than waste time on negotiations, claiming that the tribesmen had already been in limbo for the past two years, as they "do not know when they will be flooded and when they will not be flooded". He added that he felt the legislation was "very essential and should be hastened...".[23]

Lemke's proposal was met with a response from Montana Senator Wesley A. D'Ewart, who argued that "the right approach would be to enter into these negotiations before construction starts and before the project is finally approved and the first appropriation made. Then you have a time and opportunity to enter negotiations without the pressure of being flooded if you do not consent to the agreement."[24]

The chairman concurred, saying: "We ought to do these things before we go in there. It is like holding a gun at their heads afterwards."

The meeting ended with a remark made by Representative Toby Morris: "Besides that, when you take reservation land, you destroy not only the actual land that is taken, but you destroy the community life, religious and civic life of the people. You destroy nations, as a matter of fact."[25]

Time would prove him right.

Douglas White Bull, a polite, soft-spoken man of seventy-four, is the grandson of Chief White Bull, nephew of the legendary Hunkpapa Chief Sitting Bull. He joined us at our table as we sat with LaDonna on that day at the Prairie Knights Casino, and, hearing us talk about the Missouri River, started telling us about his childhood. He used to live "8 miles south of Kenel South Dakota, all along the Missouri River, big cottonwood trees, just beautiful, lot of wild game, just nice". Those were relatively good times, Doug reminisced. Early boyhood in the Plains meant childish challenges such as daring each other to swim across the Missouri River. "We hunted, wild berries – all the time, we picked up for our mother – wild turnips, and so that's what we ate." Then, "along come cluster homes," he continued, with a grim look on his face:

> when we first gave up and moved back after the battle of Little Big-horn, the government said, "Don't let them keep together, move them apart so that they don't gather". So they give us, like, 160 acres [per person][26] ... Then, all of a sudden, they started building these housing projects, so everybody moved into these cluster sites. There is where the problem started. The alcoholism, drugs, child abuse, child neglect, it goes on and on and on.

In his book *Dammed Indians*, Michael Lawson makes a similar point, relating the origins of "the problem" to a relatively new phrase coined by a group of sociologists and anthropologists: "involuntary resettlement".[27] Lawson tells us the research group that came up with the phrase had two primary concerns: to develop a socially sustainable approach to addressing the hardships faced by those forced to relocate due to massive infrastructure projects; and to formulate a plan for conflict resolution between those affected and the planners. The infrastructure projects that the group observed were larger undertakings than the Pick–Sloan Plan, Lawson points out, but at the social level their effects were similar to those of the Oahe Dam and Reservoir. Their conclusion, which also holds true for Pick–Sloan is that "development projects usually are afflicted by an engineering bias, which neglects social planning and characteristically understates the difficulties to be faced by a proposed project. They are also inclined to ignore the host population and put excessive pressure on the environment." He adds:

> projects almost universally incur construction-cost overruns at the same time that they under-finance resettlement expenses, and the number of people or families to be displaced is consistently underestimated. Finally, researchers have found that forced resettlement more often than not creates an inflated market for replacement lands, goods, and services.

This is exactly what happened in the 1950s and 1960s, when Federal Government contracts for land acquisition to construct the Oahe Reservoir were finalised. The area flooded and the people were moved. "They never built us enough houses," says LaDonna, and continues:

> The homes that they took, we owned, they belonged to us. Then they rebuilt, hut-houses belonging to the Federal Government that we cannot own. And they took all our businesses, all our stores,

everything ... In the 1970s we went through, what, economic crises. So that is where we are at right now. And then the government installed all these laws and codes and rules, so we cannot go to a bank to open a business, we cannot go to a bank to build a home, we cannot go to a bank to buy a car, anything, because we are Indians and we have tribal trust lands, so we have no collateral.

She then adds: "So why wasn't this devastating to us? Because we already lived off the land, we already had a system, a custom and a way of life."

Environmental expert Robert Schneiders contends that the real reason behind the involuntary resettlement of native communities against a backdrop of Missouri River development was largely congressional budgetary concerns. "Site selection was dependent upon geology, cost-effectiveness, demographics and political considerations," he writes.[28] "Purchasing prime agricultural land, or expensive urban real estate, would have increased the overall cost of a dam's construction,"[29] whereas the land in the reservations, considered to be "underutilized" and "low quality", would come relatively cheap. Thus, native communities were excluded from the planning process, and "on the remote reservations of the upper Missouri River, the Indian population had little or no idea that plans and policies were being formulated that would dramatically affect their lives".[30] By the time they found out that a large chunk of their reservation land was what the Pick–Sloan Plan was looking at for congressional approval, it was already too late. Schneiders, quoting Department of Interior and Bureau of Indian Affairs figures, tells us that 353,313 acres of reservation land were lost to the Pick–Sloan dams for reservoir water storage, and more than 10,000 Native Americans were affected

by the dams built along the Missouri River to varying degrees.
Those "forced to relocate from the valley lands to the uplands or
off reservation towns"[31] numbered approximately 3,500.

Today, a short paragraph tacked to the end of a webpage talking about the Pick–Sloan Plan on the National Park Service website sums up the Native American experience:[32]

> While most basin residents welcomed the Pick–Sloan Plan, not
> everyone did. American Indians, those whose reservations bor-
> dered the river, particularly opposed it. They were the biggest
> losers. The reservoirs flooded their best agricultural and grazing
> lands and displaced hundreds of families. Most affected by the
> Pick–Sloan Plan, they reaped the least benefit from it.

Not only were their homes, agricultural and grazing lands
gone, but the whirlwind that created the sacred stones had also
disappeared. "When the Army Corps came in and dredged
the mouth of the Cannonball," recalls LaDonna, "there was no
longer a whirlwind, and so the sacred stones were not made any
more." Along with the whirlwind, many other things important
to LaDonna vanished as well:

> when I was a child living in Fort Yates, we had a bakery, a motel,
> a hotel, barbershop, jewellery store, a mercantile store, a grocery
> store, a restaurant: everything, basically. And when the Army
> Corps came in to flood us, they bought out the businesses ... And
> then the Army Corps said, "I am gonna take your homes, and we
> will replace your homes"; well, the Army Corps only built and the
> Federal Government only built so much houses. So, then we had
> four, five families per house. And then it's still like that.

The nemesis: Dakota Access

With childhood memories of their lands being grabbed and their homes flooded still fresh in many people's minds, it is understandable how residents of the Standing Rock and Cheyenne River Reservations might have felt when Dakota Access came knocking: history was repeating itself. Once again, they were facing a project that would benefit a large, non-native corporation. Once again, a replanning was undertaken to minimise the effect of the project on white communities. Once again, USACE, the agency that had been brought in to grant an easement under the infamous Oahe Dam and Reservoir, was in the picture. And, once again, indigenous communities were completely left out of the consultation process.

The story of DAPL had in fact started a few years earlier. In 2014, Dakota Access, LLC, the company operating under Energy Transfer Partners that was responsible for constructing the crude oil pipeline system, made an initial application to USACE. The pipeline, once completed, would carry the "US light sweet"[33] of the Bakken and Three Forks oil fields in North Dakota to a holding facility 1,172 miles away in Patoka, Illinois.[34] The proposed pipeline, projecting expenses in the range of US$4 billion dollars, boasted an ambitious maximum carrying capacity of 570,000 barrels a day. Its originally planned route crossed underneath the Missouri riverbed, approximately 10 miles north of Bismarck: the predominantly white capital city of the state of North Dakota.

USACE conducted an initial environmental assessment, producing a 1,261 page document that they published on 25 July 2015. In this bulky report, several issues stood out. The most controversial of these was the claim that the initial route proposal was not feasible due to the proximity the pipeline would have to the municipal wells (Bismarck's major supply of drinking water), which would pose an imminent threat to public health. This, and the fact that the route would be passing through a higher number of sensitive habitats – including wildlife refuges, state trust lands and private tribal lands – would also make the planning process both more complicated and more expensive. Thus, the report noted, early in the planning phase of the project, the construction company had considered but later eliminated this alternative route. However, if undertaken, it would have originated in Stanley, North Dakota, headed "southwest through Williams County and crossed the Missouri River approximately 8.5 miles east of the Yellowstone River and Missouri River confluence", alternately heading southeast and crossing "Lake Oahe approximately 10 miles north of Bismarck". The route would then dip southerly and enter "South Dakota approximately 35 miles east of Lake Oahe in McIntosh County".[35]

The report also underlined concerns raised by the residents of Bismarck over the initial proposal, adding that following "public input and comment during this EA process" and further evaluation, elimination of "this route as a viable alternative" was decided. Taking this alternative off the table, the Corps would now focus on a new route that passed north of Cannonball and underneath the Oahe Reservoir, approximately half a mile away from the Standing Rock Sioux Reservation. According to USACE, this reroute would not have any "significant impact" on the quality of the "human environment",[36] a contention that in time would add fuel to the protests at Standing Rock.

On 18 August 2016, at the height of the demonstrations at Standing Rock Sioux Reservation, the *Bismarck Tribune* published an article[37] in which the reasons behind this change of route were detailed. For the first time, the media was echoing the concerns of the protesters, while highlighting the argument that the Standing Rock Sioux Tribe had been voicing all along: there was a different route originally proposed and later rejected. This rerouting, the Sioux believed, clearly translated into putting the interests of the predominantly white community above the indigenous one, and such a preference would soon ignite arguments over "environmental racism."[38]

The article also claimed a map was included in the Dakota Access's application to the Public Service Commission (PSC) in May 2014, which showed the original route of the pipeline passing north of Bismarck. However, among the paperwork submitted to the North Dakota PSC, no such map exists today. Instead, there exists in the archives a single map dated 11 June 2014, showing the current route skirting the northern extreme of Cannonball.[39]

With the original map missing, the North Dakota PSC defended itself through their chairperson and "pipeline siting portfolio holder" Julie Fedorchak, in a statement issued to the press on 27 October 2016. Fedorchak put the ball in USACE's court regarding the rerouting, claiming the Bismarck route was turned down by USACE and the original proposal never even made it to them:

> The river crossing north of Bismarck was a proposed alternative considered by the [Dakota Access] company early in the routing process. This route was never included in the proposed route submitted to the PSC and therefore was never vetted or considered by us during our permitting process. It had been eliminated by the U.S. Army Corps of Engineers during their environmental assessment.[40]

In December 2016, the Standing Rock Sioux Tribe posted a full sound recording of a September 2014 meeting of the Standing Rock Sioux Tribal Council, with tribal representatives from several districts in the Dakotas, the representatives of DAPL and its parent company, Energy Transfer Partners, on their YouTube channel.[41] The disclosure of this particular sound recording came in answer to comments made by Energy Transfer Partners' CEO Kelcy Warren, who spoke with several media outlets following USACE's unexpected decision to halt the construction of the pipeline until further analysis could be made to decide on an easement under the Oahe Reservoir.[42] Warren, in a 16 November 2016 article published by the *Wall Street Journal*, was quoted saying that he really wished "for the Standing Rock Sioux that they had engaged in discussions way before they did. I don't think we would have been having this discussion if they did. We could have changed the route. It could have been done, but it's too late."[43]

The *Bismarck Tribune*, while reporting on the sound recording,[44] highlighted the timing of the 2014 meeting between pipeline officials and tribal representatives. It mentioned that this meeting took place three months before Energy Transfer Partners applied for a permit with the North Dakota PSC, "and nearly [twenty] months before pipeline construction started in North Dakota".[45] Thus, the tribe's disclosure of the sound recording killed two birds with one stone: it not only proved that there existed strong tribal objection and resistance to any pipeline that would pass through what the chairman of the Standing Rock Sioux Tribal Council called "treaty boundaries",[46] but also debunked Warren's allegations that the tribe did not engage in discussions during the planning process.

With the online disclosure of this recording, the public could now hear that the company knew early on that the Standing Rock Sioux Tribe was just as averse to a pipeline coming in close proximity to their community as the residents of Bismarck had been. Throughout the hour-long meeting, company representatives sweated under a barrage of well-directed comments, explanations and questions from tribal representatives, making references to culturally and historically significant areas, sacred prayer sites and burial grounds; the fact that USACE officials had not consulted the tribe regarding these areas, and that, although they had been previously notified, they did not send any representatives to the meeting; the overall shortcomings of USACE and their permit-granting process, especially where the Standing Rock Sioux Tribe was concerned; and similar instances in the United States in which the court had ruled in favour of tribes, such as the *Delaware Riverkeeper v. the Federal Energy Regulatory Commission*. There were also questions as to how and in what capacity Energy Transfer Partners truly intended to utilise this pipeline.

Tribal Historic Preservation Officer Waste' Win Young gave a concise summary of the Standing Rock Sioux Tribe's former dealings with USACE regarding pipelines past that had crossed in close proximity to their reservation, and for which the environmental assessments made were not satisfactory from a tribal perspective. What stood out in Young's testimony was her assertion that "there are critical issues within the NHPA[47] and the NEPA[48] processes that the Army Core repeatedly overlooks, on projects where the Standing Rock Sioux Tribe has consulted on. One such concern would be the segmenting of the routes under the National Environmental Policy Act in order to streamline the permitting process." She continued to exemplify using the *Delaware Riverkeeper v. the Federal Energy Regulatory Commission* case, for which on 6 June 2014 the United States Court of Appeals ruled that "a continuous pipeline project cannot be segmented into multiple parts to avoid a comprehensive NEPA review". Young stated that USACE had followed the same problematic approach in both Keystone XL and Flanagan South Pipelines, applying streamline permits in each case. "*Delaware Riverkeeper v. FERC* dealt with breaking up a new 40-mile-long pipeline up [*sic*] into four segments," she told the room, whereas in the case of Keystone XL and Flanagan South, USACE "shape-shifted the two projects, both [of] which were hundreds of miles long into thousands of single complete projects for permitting purposes". She went on to say that now, with DAPL, USACE was once again aiming to do exactly that: "when it comes to working with tribes, especially the Standing Rock Sioux Tribe, their *modus operandi* is to streamline the process, using the Nationwide Permit 12[49] to complete smaller segments for Environmental Analysis, or the 404 permit which says their agency is only responsible to consult on their jurisdictional boundaries where the project crosses a waterway of the United States of America". This, she concluded, was "unacceptable." By the end of the meeting, the DAPL representative's declaration that lunch would now be served, a notion reminiscent of the old days of land councils, went largely amiss.

At the core of all the fighting over who was responsible for the initial rerouting of the pipeline lies the argument that the members of the Standing Rock Sioux Tribe were trying to bring to the fore in their fight against DAPL: "we are not expandable".

As the evidence clearly suggests, following objections from Bismarck residents, DAPL was rerouted, without taking into account the objections of the native communities, which would be directly affected by this new decision. The Sioux rightfully felt that, once again, they were at the mercy of a self-serving decision by USACE. The army, through its Corps of Engineers, had decided that a pipeline crossing underneath the Missouri River so close to human settlement would not constitute a threat to the "quality of the human environment", provided that this environment happened to belong to a native tribe. The same concern Bismarck's residents raised about their drinking water fell on deaf ears when voiced by members of the Sioux Nation. The question remained: if the potential risk of a leak to the municipal wells was too big to take, what made that risk any less potent if the pipeline crossed underneath Lake Oahe, the main source of drinking water for the reservation and all other human dwellings, native and non-native alike, along the Missouri River south of the reservation?

For LaDonna, the familiar turn of events was not surprising:

As indigenous people, we know these attempts to erase us very well, and one of the ways it works is through environmental racism. Indigenous lands across the country are the sites of nuclear waste dumping, toxic mining operations, oil and gas drilling, and a long list of other harmful environmental practices, but see very little benefit from these projects. We live in the sacrifice zones. And that is the story here too – the Dakota Access Pipeline was rerouted from north of Bismarck, a mostly white community, out of concerns for their drinking water, but then redirected to ours. They consider our community "expendable".[50]

BOX 2. Another exploitation en masse

What LaDonna means by environmental racism is a notion the Ramapough Lunaape Nation of northern New Jersey knows all too well. Until eight years ago, they were engaged in a similar fight against another major corporation: Ford Motor Company. Ford's now long-closed Mahwah plant dumped toxic paint sludge in and around Ringwood from 1967 up until 1971. The pollution eventually brought with it deadly diseases, including rare, incurable cancers, culminating in a lawsuit that ended in 2009 with a settlement in favour of the tribe and the communities affected. The settlement Ford would jointly pay with the Borough of Linwood, twenty-nine years after the plant closed down, amounted to US$12.5 million.[51] However, payments to individuals for their suffering were derisory, with most receiving small amounts such as US$4,000; the largest payment to any one individual was US$35,000.

Mahwah, the New Jersey town where the Ramapough Lunaape have their tribal offices, is a mere 45-minute drive from New York City. Another 15 to 20 minutes by car is necessary to reach Ringwood State Park, a popular destination for those wishing to escape Manhattan's mayhem. It is also the hotspot where, half a century ago, trucks routinely dumped thousands of tons of Ford Motor Company's toxic waste.

The entrance to the park on any given weekend is hard to miss, with a multitude of cars parked outside and parents heading into the park with their children for outdoor activities. Although the sludge marks are no longer visible along the popular walking route, this does not alter the fact that the forest has been a toxic waste bin. For someone with knowledge of this toxic history, the springs spouting idyllically from the ground between the trees and rocks only serve as reminders of the poison that for decades seeped into the streams and lakes, and of the water that still continues to contaminate all that lies in its path.

The Ramapough Lunaape are a widely misunderstood and misrepresented tribe from the Ramapough Mountains. Due to the limited number of acquired white-men surnames that the tribal members hold today, they have been the subject of unfounded speculation regarding inbreeding, while their worship practices and sacred sites are often the centrepieces of local folklore. Further adding to their frustration, they have been portrayed as foul and degenerate characters in mainstream television series.

"They say we're an isolated mountain tribe, but we're only on this mountain because we retreated here," Dwaine Perry, Chief of the Ramapough Lunaape Nation, explained in a rare interview with a New Jersey newspaper exactly one year before the protests at Standing Rock. "We were farmers, but got driven off our land when the Europeans came."[52]

The injustices the Ramapough Lunaape have been forced to bear are crowned by the ironic fact that the site on which the Ford plant was built formerly acted as ceremonial grounds for their tribe.[53] This sacred place of worship has become a source of toxicity that is now slowly killing them.

The battle to clean up Ringwood continues to this day. Details of the pollution, the legal battle, the threats to the community to withdraw their complaints and the ongoing health issues faced by the residents of Ringwood and Ramapough have been turned into a digital archive by the North Jersey newspaper *The Record*, available to access as an interactive

website titled *Toxic Legacy*.[54] What stands out in this extensive reportage and documentation is the fact that, once again, a
poor, largely native community is seemingly powerless to prevent polluted waste being dumped on it, all the while facing
intimidatory tactics. *The Record* asserts that "Organized Crime
played a key role in a vast assault on the environment. An analysis of public records and interviews with truckers who hauled
Ford's waste shows mob-controlled contractors dumped anywhere they could get away with it. They bribed, threatened,
even murdered to maintain control of Ford's trash."[55]

Across the United States, the resistance native communities
such as the Ramapough have shown against big money, which
has formerly gained little coverage in the media, is now becoming visible thanks to Standing Rock. Since the early days of the
"No-DAPL" protests at Standing Rock, several petition sites
have sprung up across the internet advocating the Ringwood
story.[56] Inspired by the events unfolding in the Great Plains,
the Ramapough Lunaape, along with other indigenous nations,
are now finding new ways (such as internet advocacy) and
rediscovering the old (such as igniting old-school journalism)
to make their voices heard. Thus, the real fight against what
LaDonna calls "environmental racism" is just beginning.

TWO | Seventh Generation

We really do see ourselves as part of a community, the immediate commu-
nity, the Native American community, but part of your nation and the
Confederacy. And if you have been given responsibilities within that struc-
ture, you must really attend to those responsibilities. You start to think in
terms of the people who come after me. Those faces that are coming from
beneath the earth that are yet unborn, is the way we refer to that. They
are going to need the same things that we have found here, they would
like the earth to be as it is now, or a little better. Everything that we have
now is the result of our ancestors who handed forth to us our language,
the preservation of the land, our way of life and the songs and dances. So
now we will maintain those and carry those on for future generations.
(G. Peter Jemison, Faithkeeper, Cattaraugus Reservation of the Seneca
Nation)

If you ask me what is the most important thing that I have learned about
being a Haudenosaunee, it's the idea that we are connected to a commu-
nity, but a community that transcends time.

We're connected to the first Indians who walked on this earth, the very
first ones, however long ago that was. But we're also connected to those
Indians who aren't even born yet, who are going to walk this earth. And
our job in the middle is to bridge that gap. You take the inheritance from
the past, you add to it, your ideas and your thinking, and you bundle it

up and shoot it to the future. And there is a different kind of responsibility. That is not just about me, my pride and my ego, it's about all that other stuff. We inherit a duty, we inherit a responsibility. And that's pretty well drummed into our heads. Don't just come here expecting to benefit. You come here to work hard so that the future can enjoy that benefit. (Rick Hill Sr. (Tuscarora) Chair, Haudenosaunee Standing Committee on NAGPRA)[1]

I want to bring change to each home, to each heart, mind and soul throughout this world. To whoever will read this, I just want to say no matter where you come from or who you are, I stand with you my brother and sister. I will stand for your struggles, I will stand for your accomplishments but most of all, I will stand for your life. We all deserve to live the best life that we can! Mitakuye Oyasin![2] (Bobbi Jean Three Legs, Standing Rock Sioux Tribe)[3]

The Seventh Generation take control at Standing Rock

Bobbi Jean Three Legs will be twenty-five years old in a couple of weeks, but she doesn't show her age at all. She is tall and beautiful, and when looking at her energetic and youthful manners, you need to continuously remind yourself that she is already a mother of a three year old and almost done with her Associates Degree in Criminal Justice. In addition to all of the responsibilities she carries on her shoulders, Bobbi Jean is also a long-distance runner and, being such, she became a messenger for the No-DAPL movement.

"She is my hero," says LaDonna as she introduces her. "She is the one who first started walking and running and organising. So she's with a bunch of youth here, they have been working really hard." She points towards a long table behind us, where a bunch of young people from both the Standing Rock and Cheyenne River Reservations are sitting down to eat. When they see us looking at them, they all turn around, smile and cheerfully wave at us.

After the founding of Sacred Stone in April, the word needed to be spread, the message carried across, to raise awareness. People needed to be told why the Standing Rock Sioux Tribe stood in opposition to Dakota Access. So, Bobbi Jean chose a method of doing so that came naturally to her, one that she carried in her blood, inherited from her ancestors: running.

Since precolonial times, tribes across the Americas carried messages by way of runners: a special group of people who were trained from early childhood in long-distance running. These messengers were required not only to endure long-distance running to reach their destination, but also to shoulder the important responsibility of carrying the messages entrusted to them across in their original version. A sharp memory was needed to remember the oral messages word-for-word and deliver them in their exact form.

So, when her tribe was confronted with a direct threat to their livelihood, Bobbi Jean decided to do what she had trained for all her life: run, talk to people, interact with them and carry the message across and out of the boundaries of the Standing Rock Sioux Reservation. She first pooled together a group of about thirty runners, mostly young people: "The first run, it was only 11.1 miles," she says, and it encouraged them to continue. "The second run was 500-mile relay run", which took them from Cannonball all the way to Omaha, where they hoped to deliver their message to the USACE. The message explicitly stated that they did not want an easement to be granted to DAPL to cross under-neath the Oahe Reservoir. Throughout these "water-runs", as the media would soon label them, the group grew in size, but the core members of the group always stayed the same.

After Omaha, the runners' next plan was an ambitious stretch covering the distance between Cannonball, North Dakota and Washington DC: "We just say 2000, but I'm not, I don't know the accurate numbers," Bobbi says. "The second run took us eight days, and the third run took us twenty-eight days." In that last run, some of the participants would see the capital city of the United States for the first time in their lives. The whole experi-ence – coming out of their reservations and seeing the big cities – was, Bobbi reflects, for most of them "kind of a culture shock. Especially cos we live out in open prairies. And going into cities, where you have these massive huge buildings, you can't even see the sunrise or the sunset, you can't really see nature in cities."

As Bobbi tells us her story of the water-runs, LaDonna cannot help but join in on the conversation to stress that the youngest of the runners was a four-month-old baby, her mother being a run-ner, who accompanied the group for the entire distance.

When we talk about those days of the camps being set up at Standing Rock, and the water-runs, Bobbi believes, "the best part out of, probably out of all the experiences put together, is educating the people about Standing Rock. Because people have this idea that us, Native Americans, still live in tipis, or they don't really think we are modernised, living-wise, I guess." So, first they had to try to overcome that hurdle, and explain themselves to correct this misinformation. The way they accomplished it was through "pretty much just sharing our stories with them, our life stories too, the generational trauma that all of us went through, the hardships". She adds, "everyone was on a one-on-one talk, sometimes I'd get really personal with them, just kinda help them understand more. I always went back further generations, with my grandmothers' generation all the way up to my generation, and everything that we all went through."

LaDonna, soon after founding Sacred Stone, cried out to the world asking people to come, and they did. This Bobbi took one step further, organising her fellow runners to go directly to the people instead of waiting for them to show up at Standing Rock. She says, "it was more of something that we just literally had to do, cos we didn't have any choice but to stand up". She was correct in assuming this, considering that historically it has been the Federal Government's tendency to draw a curtain around the reservations and silence any resistance as they wrestle what they want out of the hands of the native communities: much like they did during the land commissions following the Sioux Bill of 1889.[4]

G. E. Hyde gives a detailed account of this period, in which tribesmen were once again being hustled into signing documents for the Sioux Land Commission of 1889, and "officials were headed down the road that led to the use of trickery and frontier shakedown methods". We read of fearmongering and outright threats being used as techniques to grab nine million acres from the Sioux Nation by members of the Commission, including high-ranking army officials – such as Major General George Crook – whom the Sioux had once fought against. The Federal Government in Washington, again deaf to any opposition coming from the tribes, had fallen in line with the demands of its white voter base. Thus, "much as they might oppose the sale of their lands, the 25,000 Sioux could not hold out much longer against the pressure exerted by the 500,000 whites in Dakota, who were trying to get the Indian lands".[5] Fastforward to the present day, and there is not much of an attitude change. The Federal Government with its branches and agencies is once again deaf to protests by tribes, and when native interests lie opposed to those of its white voter base, it chooses to accommodate the latter.

So, for the tribes in the Great Plains, those days of land commissions and treaties are not far gone. Even with this much colonial history in mind, and with its marks still painfully visible, one cannot help but wonder if Bobbi and her friends realised at the time what a big mission they were taking upon their shoulders. Through the outreach from the water-runs and their coverage on conventional and social media, the potential curtain of silence was lifted, and the world knew once and for all where Standing Rock stood.

However, a dream that Bobbi had before "all this happened" may further help the reader to understand what DAPL means to native communities who lay in its direct path. Bearing in mind that the realm of dreams is sacred for the Native Americans, Bobbi tells us of the dream she had "probably a few weeks or a month before" the water-runs took place and the camps were set up at Standing Rock. At the time, she says, she did not ponder it too much. However, when looking back on it today, all of its parts fall perfectly into place:

> I had this dream, of our river being on fire. Like our whole river was on fire. I was driving, cos, where we live, the river just [is] like right beside the road, and I was driving, and I was looking, and I was looking out to the river and just on top was literally on fire.

And you could tell that it was oil because, remember, oil floats on top of water. And the sky was just all dark, and grey, like smoky.

She pauses before adding: "I never really had dreams like that before; then all this happened."

For young people, taking charge in a situation and speaking up isn't exactly something that falls in line with native tradition. Speaking up in society or speaking out in council, making decisions and carrying them forward is not encouraged in the young when the elders are present. So, when in Standing Rock the youth took charge after their elders had paved the way, it was a noteworthy moment. Bobbi says the movement helped her find her voice. Now when she speaks in front of large crowds, "it all flows out and it feels really good not to have to be compressed with all my life stories and all, whatever we went through, that my family went through, that my people went through. Just to be able to talk." She adds that this new outspokenness is "really healing" her.

LaDonna encourages Bobbi by saying she believes in her, and that she will be a very successful motivational speaker one day. The young woman nods and says that she really has found out that she likes talking, and Standing Rock has helped her find her path in life. "I had these two ladies come up to me in camp, or these two sisters, and they are probably, I wanna say, maybe, ten years older than me, in their late thirties," she tells us:

They just came up, and want to introduce themselves, and then they were telling me their stories of trauma and everything that they went through. And they told me that they never talked about that before with anybody, or even talked about it with their own siblings or their family. And I guess when they heard me talk one time, that just like kinda made them think and open up.

So there they stood, talking about their individual experiences. "Pretty soon, it was like an hour and a half later, we were still standing there, and I got to hear both of their stories," Bobbi tells us. "It was really inspiring."

Meanwhile, down at the Cheyenne River

Time literally changes as you cross the Lake Oahe Bridge into the Cheyenne River Reservation. Although the cell signal in this area is weak, as soon as it picks up a couple of bars, the clock on your smartphone immediately jumps back one hour. This carries symbolic resonances as you continue to drive through the plains and wide, open ranches towards the heart of the reservation. Eagle Butte, a small strip town acting as the main hub, looks frozen in time. The aptly named Main Street, which cuts through the center, hosts most of the town's necessities: a gas station, a market, the Lakota Cultural Center, the only two motels on the reservation, and a store that carries pretty much everything else, including yards of fabric with buffalo designs on them. Off Main Street lies a large, old building that differentiates Cheyenne River from all other reservations in the Great Plains: this is home to the Cheyenne River Youth Project, or CRYP, the sound of which is similar to "crib" when spoken aloud, and thus stands for its purpose.

A civil initiative, the Youth Project has been in existence since 1988. Julie Garreau, a Miniconjou Lakota and an enrolled member of the Cheyenne River Sioux Tribe, is the founder of the Project and executive director of the youth centre that serves as its base. She tells us that before she secured the building from the tribal government, it used to be a bar. Now as you enter it, it is a colourful, cheerful safe haven for kids.

Julie clearly remembers those early days in 1988 when she founded CRYP and later tried to get the premises to realise her dream: "Kids needed a place to go. It was really simple. It wasn't complicated, I wasn't complicated, the project wasn't complicated." With only that dream in mind, she asked for the building, "The Main", as it was to the community up until then:

> they were really open to the idea because there just wasn't anything in our community for that. I think it was a major statement to take an old bar and turn it into a youth centre, which, at the time, you know, alcohol, which still plagues our nation, which is still a cause of why we lose people, our people. People are dying.

After a brief pause, she adds, "I thought that was a really good statement to go ahead and say we are closing this bar, and we are gonna turn it into something positive, and beautiful, and when you look at where we began, and you see where we are now, it's kind of remarkable. It really is."

Just as The Main transformed into CRYP, over the years the centre has also transformed the lives of many young people, both the youth who have come through its doors and its staff: healing most, teaching the rest. It has not all been easy, though. Tammy Joy Granados is the Youth Programmes Director for the Project, and she has been with CRYP for ten years. She remembers the day she came to the centre for her job interview. Burnt out from classes and exams in her final year of college, Tammy saw an article in the newspaper "that was asking for a Youth Programmes Assistant for the Cheyenne River Youth Project, and I said, 'well, I need the job'", and so she applied. "I had no idea who Cheyenne River Youth Project was," she confesses before explaining further: "We call it The Main. If you are from here, if you are local, this isn't the Cheyenne River Youth Project, this is 'The Main'. The original building was on Main Street and then it just became The Main. We're over here, we are still The Main. I worked here ten years, we're still The Main," she laughs:

> So I had no idea what Cheyenne River Youth Project was. I applied because I knew I would get it. I was in my senior year of the social work programme, I was gonna be done, I only had one semester of actual classes left, and I thought 'well, I'm tired of being broke, I have been broke for years, I'll apply', and I knew, just because I knew they would give it to me.

At the time, Tammy was not sure if working with youth at CRYP was the path she wanted to take. A survivor of sexual abuse as a child, she tells us that, back then, she was more interested in trauma counselling and working in emergency rooms. But from the moment she came for her interview at the youth centre until now, she has stayed. She remembers the Project having a volunteer programme in those days, "where people [came] in from all over the world to support our youth programming". That, while a blessing, was also a curse:

> there wasn't, there is never anything that's consistent. Our kids never saw a stable, consistent face. Julie: Julie was our stable, consistent face, no others. So, the idea was to create somebody who

did what the volunteers do but to be here, and to be stable, and to be consistent, and that's what I was; that's what I became at that time.

CRYP may have served the youth in the community, but the community as a whole needed healing. Tammy, whether or not she realised it at the time, needed to heal as well. And now, looking back, she believes CRYP has helped her not only to do that, but also to grow as a person. She explains:

> you grow up here, and you don't know what you don't know. You don't know any different. You don't know what happy relationships look like, you don't know that you are not in a healthy relationship. You don't know that this is not how things are supposed to go. You don't know that you deserve peace, that you deserve calm and you deserve to be safe, and you don't know those things because you've never had different. Sometimes your parents never had different. Your friends don't have different, you're like, you don't know that you deserve better.

Reflecting on her personal experience, she adds: "I didn't know. I read all these textbooks, and I was taking all these classes, and I was learning all these things, but it never had really addressed, I suppose, the emotional and all, and the mental part of me. It was books, it was textbooks, it was … it was outside of me."

At CRYP, however, what went on was very real.

Helping the youth help themselves

When we arrived at the youth centre, the staff were distressed, as their supply closet had been broken into and a bunch of material had been stolen the night before. What seemed to be missing were mainly cleaning supplies, which Julie believed pointed to drug dealers. Already late for her meeting in Rapid City, she chose to delay her leave, stay a couple more hours and talk to her team about how to handle further potential break-ins. When I later asked her about the difficulties she ran into while working with youth at CRYP, she candidly shared her concerns:

> I feel like a lot of the same issues are there from twenty years ago. Which is, you have a community where there is an extreme amount of dysfunction, and you can absolutely relate a lot of what has happened to our families in our communities because of the forced assimilation, the colonisation: all that historical trauma really has impacted what's happening today. And that is not an easy thing to solve, and take care of, or remove.

She shrugged and resumed with renewed enthusiasm: "So, you know, we are working at it just little piece at a time. The impact we have with kids is probably after parental and family impact, and then the school has a piece of it, and then we get to be a part of their lives too."

Despite these "same issues", as Julie calls them, being carried forward in time, the devil is in the detail:

> when I started this work, the big conversations were about the drugs of choice at that point, which were marijuana, and things like that, and alcohol of course still being an issue. Now, we have meth that is taking control of our community. It's overwhelming to think about what meth is doing. And it is happening [to] a lot of native

communities. But it happens really to rural communities because the drug is so easy to make, and the ingredients you can buy in your local stores.

Ingredients similar to the material stolen from them the night before.

As we sat in the youth centre's small meeting room, our host paused for a while, then turned and asked Tammy, "I don't really know about the price of meth. You know anything about that? Is it expensive?", to which Tammy replied, "not much, like five bucks. For a high." Julie then turned back to us and continued, "it's cheap. It's cheap for a high." Thoughtful, she explained, "you know the fact that we are a Sovereign Nation, I think we are also a target for cartels and people who wanna bring drugs in. I think that there is a big movement now between the Federal Government and the Tribal Governments to really begin to work on this issue." However, the fact that meth is so easy and cheap to make, she said, and thus so easily found, made her feel desperate: "I still sit around thinking 'I don't know what to do about meth'. I really don't." She kept on pondering: "I mean, it is so big and it is so scary, so hard to treat and it is, it's really overwhelming." She continued to explain:

I have family who have taken that path, I know that. So it is a pretty tough route to take for someone and often you don't get back. You don't come back. Unless somebody's there with you walking you through the process, and helping you, because, you know, I have talked to people who have been a part of meth, and what they tell you is that once meth is in your community, it will always be there. But they also say that the craving, and the longing for it is always there. It's lifelong, even if you are off.

Without a support system, backsliding is inevitable, Julie stressed. With a support system, however, "whether it is a circle of family or friends, or some sort of institution that can support you," things might begin to look up.

And, as hard as it is, at CRYP they aim to offer just that.

A chance to heal

Julie's concern over the growing rates of meth addiction in reservations was something that also hit home for LaDonna back in Standing Rock. In June 2015, Prairie McLauglin, LaDonna's only daughter, was run over by a car. The driver was a young meth addict and would soon plead guilty to driving under the influence to get a reduced sentence.

Sitting inside the casino back in April 2017, LaDonna told us Prairie's story prior to the accident. When her son, Philip, passed away, it was her daughter Prairie who took in his sons. "So, my daughter Prairie, she has six children she is raising," LaDonna said. She then mentioned Prairie's daughter and LaDonna's only granddaughter, Skye: "I raised her," she added proudly, before telling us about the hardships her daughter had to put up with in life, "not because of anything she did, because of circumstances." It pretty much started with her daughter's house catching fire, a trauma that Prairie still fights with today, as "her and the kids lost everything." However, the young woman had as much fight in her as her mother. Having lost everything, and with no one to help her, she rebuilt her house single-handedly, LaDonna told us: "remodelled the whole thing herself."

But Prairie's misfortunes wouldn't end there. While trying to put her life back on track, in June 2015, the young woman had the accident. "His little brother was in the street and a car sped by," LaDonna recalled of that day, pointing at Joshua, her grandson, who was still sitting with us at the table. Prairie grabbed the small boy, pulled him off the street and into safety, and then "turned around and started yelling at that guy: 'Slow down!' And so he spun his car around, and he came at her, hit her straight on." Prairie was airlifted to Bismark, reportedly suffering from a fractured skull along with a broken collarbone, arm and leg. Despite having a long recovery period ahead of her, LaDonna said her daughter continued working, keeping herself busy by taking care of the kids and the garden. "She was in so much pain. But she just continued working," LaDonna added, the pride she felt for her daughter's perseverance apparent.

Later, Prairie mentioned these same events in our online chats, which stretched over a few days. She said that she was in so much physical pain that she was practically living off pain killers. The whole ordeal would prove to be a rough ride for the entire family. In July 2015, a month after the accident, LaDonna made an entry on her Facebook account: "Yesterday I watched my daughter cry again because each doctor appointment we hear more news about her injuries, they casted [sic] her broken arm yesterday, I worry because she still cares for five children, a house, animals, and she feels so helpless." To top it all off, they would soon receive news that the driver who ran Prairie over would "be tried in children's court". The grief-stricken mother continued: "[I]f the court give this boy a slap on the hand I know our system has failed, we are in trouble, our people are at the mercy of the drug culture. Our people are being held hostage to drugs, you can see the people who use pain pills, and drugs. Why are we so damaged?" Despite the apparent desperation, she tried to end her entry on a higher note: "I still believe in order to save the people we must know our culture, way of life, language, history and spirituality to survive into the future. Our way of life is about healing self and we all need that. I need to work on myself and start those prayers for this young man and his brother. Pray for all his family that they will find the peace in their lives."

Unsurprisingly, when Standing Rock happened Prairie naturally became an integral part of the movement. "I was there before it all started," she told me in an online interview I had with her a few months after I visited the Dakotas. "We knew what we were going into when this all started." She continued, "we've never spoken to media, my friends are still silent". However, Prairie decided to break her silence. So, as we were preparing this book for print, she told me that she was ready to talk about the early days of their efforts to reverse the decision on DAPL, when they were desperately attempting to obtain reliable information and trying to have their voices heard.

"My mother, she protects me," Prairie said on that first day we chatted via an unreliable internet connection that kept going down. However, she was a fighter, and was in need of little protection. Healing, however, was a different matter. For all of these grievances within the reservations – the drug addictions, the violence, the suffering – Standing Rock would offer a space in time, a pause of sorts, even a chance for many to start healing themselves. In Prairie's case, she took matters into her own hands, and before she was fully recovered, way before the camps had opened up, she started following all of the meetings regarding DAPL.

"August 2015 is when we started to organise against DAPL, and we started the Dakota Access opposition meetings, which we held in each district on Standing Rock. There are eight districts.

So, if you can imagine the hell we went through," she said, before adding that they accomplished all of this "on pennies and nickels". Prairie and her friends wouldn't stop with the district meetings either. They also attended Tribal Council meetings, Prairie stressed, and went "to every oil and gas meeting in the state of North Dakota". After a brief pause, she reflected, "in fact, I'm the only one that went to the oil and gas meetings in North Dakota *and* the Tribal Council meetings".

LaDonna pointed out on that day back in North Dakota that, throughout the process, the camps and the activism, Prairie "became her own person and healed herself. And still maintaining. My grandsons are on her row and all doing good; I went down because she was gone so much, and Prairie is out there, and Prairie's dad is taking care of the kids, and I was like, 'You guys wanna come and stay at Grandma's?'. They said, 'No, we are not leaving Aunt Prairie.'" Throwing her hands in the air, she added with a soft laugh, "I was like, 'OK'."

That incorrigible poverty

"Poverty has a profound effect on family structure and self-esteem, which contributes to a variety of social ills," states the CRYP website.[6] Poverty rates in reservations are close to four times those in other counties, or the overall rate for the entire state. In Sioux County, for instance, there is a concerning 40.4% poverty rate, with a median household income of US$32,895; respectively, the highest and the lowest in the state of North Dakota. The State overall hosts a 10.7% average poverty rate and a median household income of US$61,674.[7]

When going through the census data for 2015, a similar pattern exists: a widening gap in both median household income and the rate of poverty between Sioux County, of which Standing Rock Sioux Reservation is a part, and its neighbouring counties. According to 2015 data published by the US Census Bureau, in Burleigh (home to Bismarck), the rate of poverty is 9%, with a median household income of US$66,057. In Morton County, bordering Burleigh and to the north of Sioux County, the rate of poverty is 7.8%, with a median household income of US$64,260. In Grant County, on the western border of Sioux County, the rate of poverty is 15.6%, with a median household income of US$40,879. Finally, in Emmons County, bordering east, the rate of poverty is 13.9%, with a median household income of US$46,952.

Stuck in communes of low-income housing, projects, inescapable poverty, rampant alcohol and drug abuse, and inevitable suicides: these are the facts of life for many Native Americans confined to tight reservation lands, with no prospects for the future and very little hope. A lack of direction or purpose in life, coupled with depression, is the single most important factor behind the sharply inclining suicide rate among the native population, especially the young people in North America. According to data published by the Centers for Disease Control and Prevention (CDC), it is the eighth leading cause of death among Native Americans including Alaska Natives across all ages. Among the youth aged between ten and thirty-four years, it appears to be the second leading cause of death. If we compare this with the national average for the age group ranging from fifteen to thirty-four, the rate of suicide among the native population is 1.5 times higher. CDC facts also disclose that the rate of having suicidal thoughts in young adults aged eighteen and older over the one-year span leading up to their reporting was 4.8%, the highest rate across all ethnicities.[8]

Suicide as an epidemic is not a stranger to Cheyenne River either. "Suicide is always a big issue," Tammy tells us. "You talk to our IHS[9] system: 175 attempts a week is what they call it." They are only attempts, but these attempts in and of themselves descry serious suicidal behaviour, such as "drinking too much, or over-dosing on drugs," she adds. However, it was much worse when she was growing up, she recalls. "The suicide conclusions in youth were enormous when I was in high school," she continues:

> Those were my peers, those were my class mates, those were my friends at that time, because that's what age I was then. One of them was a great, great, dear friend of mine. And when I was in school, nothing, we had nothing. You know, you have nothing, you start drinking early. I started drinking when I was twelve years old, not because of anything but because, what else? And nobody is telling you anything different. And it's probably, it's a small town.

She pauses, before she concludes with a distant look: "it's small town, it's rural, it is isolated".

In 2005, when the Senate Committee on Indian Affairs held a session on suicide among American Indian youths, several tribal members with different areas of experience and expertise were invited to participate: Twila Rough Surface, member of the Standing Rock Sioux Tribe and family member of suicide vic-tims; Dr Joseph B. Stone, member of the Blackfeet Tribe and a psychologist; and Julie, representing CRYP, all testified before the Committee.[10] The hearing was aimed at addressing the increased suicide rate among young Native Americans.

Twila had lost a nephew in a car accident, an event that was followed by at least three other suicides, including that of her niece, two of her nephew's friends, and an attempted suicide by her sister: "I recently lost a niece to suicide on February 2, 2005," she testified. "She was my sister's third child," and she was twenty-three years old. Twila went on to describe the events she believed had contributed to the eventual death of her niece. "The following events," she divulged:

On January 7 of this year, her brother, my nephew, was killed in a car accident. During the grieving period, her mother had nobody to come and talk to her regarding the death of her son. So, I can only speculate that my niece saw all the hurt and could not handle the loss, so she decided to take her own life. My sister was overwhelmed by the deaths, and also tried to take her own life.

Twila relayed to the Committee what her sister had told her: "She thought that the only way to make the hurt go away was to take her life, so she would not feel the pain and the hurt." A family member had found her sister just in time and saved her life, but the effect of her nephew's death did not stay confined to the family. One of her nephew's close friends, the pallbearer at the young man's funeral, committed suicide on the same day his friend was buried. On 7 April, two months after the funeral, another one of the boy's friends also committed suicide. Twila testified that the victim was "his other best friend, he missed him very much and he was talking to my brother and he said he missed him a lot".

A lack of grief counselling, let alone psychological counselling, is one of the catalysts of these kinds of chain suicides in Twila's community. In her testimony, she stressed this very fact:

the effects of the deaths in my family have touched many and continue to be a concern. I must mention that at no point did any
mental health professionals contact our family. I feel that if there
had been intervention with grief counselling and support for my
sister and her children, my niece may have had a chance to grow
to be an elder of the community.

Dr Joseph B. Stone, representative of the American Psychological Association, a practising psychologist in Oregon and
Washington and a registered member of the Blackfeet Tribe of
Northern Montana, backed these claims by stating that he also
believed limited social services, grief counselling and mental
health services were available through Indian Health Services
(IHS) to members of native tribes residing in reservations. In his
testimony, he highlighted that they were inadequate at best, and,
at worst – considering suicide-prevention measures, for instance
– lacking entirely.

Before Dr Stone continued to give examples of the chain
suicides he'd dealt with as a professional, he pointed out the
underlying causes of these premature deaths: specifically, historical trauma. He argued that "post-colonial stress", which native
communities were suffering under, seemed to be directly inter-
fering with the capacity of children born into these societies to be
physically and mentally alert. It exhibited itself as a lack of hope
and purpose in life, while affecting the ability of their parents
and other family members – who were equally effected – to help
their children. What Dr Stone was trying to say was simple: while
growing up, if a child is continuously surrounded by feelings of
grief, depression, helplessness and similar behaviours in their
elders, who have in turn been suffering from chronic stress, then

that child's "behavioural immunity" will be compromised. This in turn manifests itself as a "lack of resilience to issues like suicide and other mental health disorders".

Historical trauma reveals itself in different ways. While Doug White Bull blames reservation life for the many ills that haunt Native Americans today, including addiction, sexual abuse and rampant suicides, Tammy believes it goes further than that:

> I think the piece of that comes down to is, when you think about a colonised people and what it means to be colonised, and what it means to be put in this certain place, and the fact that our babies were taken, the boarding schools, and were subjected to the sexual abuses; you know, those dehumanising treatments.

She goes on to add that all of those maltreatments ended up becoming part of a new generation of people, "who grew up just knowing abuse. They didn't know love, they didn't know compassion, they didn't know understanding. All they knew was abuse."

Tammy says that abuse, both physical and psychological, resulted in:

> not so much a dehumanised generation but definitely a very broken, very, very hurt generation of people, who they themselves went out and had children. Whom they didn't know how to parent and love because they were never parented and loved, wouldn't know that sexual abuse was wrong. Because the people who were telling you what was right were the people who were doing this to you.

People such as missionaries and schoolmasters all the way up to representatives of the Federal Government. Therefore, she believes, "what was done to us in the past echoes and echoes and echoes and echoes and sexual abuse is just a piece of that".

The suicides and the addiction are just two of the echoes of these historic wounds.

BOX 3. Suicide as an epidemic

In 2005, according to CDC data, the number of suicides among non-Hispanic Native Americans of both sexes was 15.08%. When the same specifications are submitted to the database for all races and both sexes for that same year, the overall rate is reported as 11.04%. To break this down into numbers, for all races and both sexes the number of suicides recorded in 2005 was 32,637 out of a national population of 295,516,599, while the number of deaths in the non-Hispanic Native American population, both sexes, was 370 out of a population pool of 2,452,970.

In 2012, Alexandra Fuller, a reporter for the monthly magazine *National Geographic*, visited Pine Ridge Reservation to cover the chronic problems haunting reservation life: omnipresent poverty, inherent substance abuse and – maybe the most painful manifestation of the demons haunting the native communities – the teenage suicide epidemic. Her article, which ran on August 2012, was titled In the Shadow of Wounded Knee. Here is an excerpt from Alexandra's account of visiting the wake of a fifteen-year-old Oglala Lakota girl:

> Partly because time is not linear for the Oglala Lakota but rather is expressed in circular endlessness and beginnings, and partly because many can recite the members of their family trees, branch after branch, twig after twig, vines and incidental outgrowths

included, it does not seem to me too big a historical step to go from the bodies piled in the snow at Wounded Knee in 1890 to the body of Dusti Rose Jumping Eagle lying in shiny mannequin perfection in an open coffin in a tepee in Billy Mills Hall in the town of Pine Ridge in early July 2011, a scarf draped over her neck to conceal the manner of her suicide.[11]

A trauma called education

Tammy tells us that her grandparents were from the boarding school era: "assimilation worked on some people really, really well," she says. "My mom was not raised in an indigenous environment. She was the only native in her school system." Her grandfather, concerned for the safety of his children, abandoned the native way of life:

He said, "we are not doing that, I don't want anybody to hurt you". He didn't speak the language. He said, "this is what is going to make them happy, this is what is going to keep us safe, this is what we're gonna do". And that's what he did with his kids, you know. My mom knows nothing about her cultural background. She couldn't pass anything onto me, but it wasn't her fault. My grandfather was full-blood Dakota, my grandmother was a full-blood Lakota, but because of what they experienced in boarding schools, they were not gonna pass on, so that their children would have to deal with that. They were gonna speak English, they were gonna live "white", they were gonna do what was expected of them so that they could live safe lives.

But it did not exactly work out the way Tammy's grandfather planned. "Yeah, it didn't come out that way. When you take away somebody's identity and you don't have anything to replace it in a manner that makes sense, you just have a lot of lost, broken people. And lost, broken people who are having more lost, broken people," she explains, the process creating a vicious cycle of hurt. To break that cycle, Tammy believes:

> you have to heal people. You have to inform them and arm them, because there are a lot of mental and emotional things that have to be fixed. You know when it comes to our communities, I, no way, believe we need money. I don't believe we need charity. I don't believe we need any of that. We need to help ourselves and hearts heal. That's where our problem lies, really.

She pauses before going on to explain: "we live in impoverished areas and we have the same problems that any impoverished area has," she tells us. "We live in a rural environment that doesn't allow, or have much resources involved in," schemes such as social programmes, and so, "you know, self-medicating is, that's what we do. That's what you do, or else you have to live with those pains and where are those pains gonna go?" she ponders. "There is nobody teaching you. How to put them anywhere else or how to deal with them or what you do with that," she painstakingly expounds. "[T]here is none of that. It's just a lot of, just a lot of hurt people who are hurting people."

Douglas White Bull also remembers his days in the boarding school as if they were yesterday: "they suppressed our spirituality, they suppressed our language," he says. "[T]he welfare department took us out, shipped us out in buses." He tells us how he ended up in a town he had never seen before in his life, 150 miles away from his home, where he was forced to stay for nine months, "and if you crossed that place, you got beat up, spanked and stuff. We talked Lakota. You tell your friend, 'Ko-aa-ahiyo', 'What did you say? Wash your mouth', so, [they] spank you, cut our hair short."

LaDonna's memories of the boarding school experience are not much different. Her pre-school life during childhood was already a tough one, she tells us, with her mother leaving them when they were little, and the children switching between foster care and relative care: not exactly an easy, steady life for a small child. At some point, when the children briefly moved in with their grandmother, all of a sudden, a rare magical period began.

"Grandma's house was great," LaDonna tells us, "we lived with Ricky." Ricky, a raccoon that lived in LaDonna's grandmother's house, was a nanny of sorts for them she tells us: "So, every morning, I always remember that, we laid in bed, and Grandma would get up early in the morning, put wood in the wood stove and get us up, and Ricky would come and pull our covers off and slap us up, and get up and then you take off." For a small child, living in peace with animals and nature as well as a grandmother who lovingly took care of you must have been extraordinary. "Those were good times at Grandma's," LaDonna reminisces, "and then they came and took us." She then continues to tell us how she was taken by the church and "put in with this school in Massachusetts, and in high school in Vermont, and then my dad was able to get me home".

Throughout her schooling, her father had struggled to gain full custody of his children; however, it would not become a reality until LaDonna was fifteen years old. All that lay between her happy childhood and her teenage years was a nightmarish period of boarding school memories: "I went to boarding school when I was in first and second [grade], that's when I learned of the devil's child," she explains. "Most of my family is left-handed. And the Catholic church forbid left-handed people, that's when I was a devil's child."

This warranted her punishment. As conservative Christians associated the left hand with the devil, LaDonna was locked up and left in a closet until she relinquished left-hand writing and adhered to the "good Christian norm". This superstition unfortunately exists to this day, with devout Christians still trying to beat left-handedness out of their children. Thus, in comparison, her pre-school days were, as hard as they were, the best times of her life: "So, in Grandma's house, nobody ever yelled at you. Nobody ever hit you, spank you, nobody ever said no to you, and every moment of the day Grandma told you she loved you, and you were great and all this stuff. And then you went to boarding school where they beat you and locked you [up]."

According to LaDonna, the idea behind the schooling of Native American children was:

to break down the culture, and the only way you can break down the culture is remove the children from their families. So, if you were Indian, you weren't raised by your families. And then they teach you everything about your culture is bad, evil, wrong, devil worshipping, whatever. And what is that word they used to teach us when we were kids – "white makes right", so we were taught this whole process and yet we come home, and life is different at home.

As Doug recounts his memories of the boarding school era, the mild-mannered old man grows unnaturally angry: "If you don't believe me, you can go up to the national archives in Washington DC where they saved all their letters and stuff," he says, urging

us to look up the correspondence regarding the forced schooling of native children. He then goes on to say that, in "the early
part, they had the church helping the government, so they are in
between: 'So, what are they doing now? How are they doing?'
'We don't know, we don't let them to do this, we don't let them
to do that, so they are behaving themselves', and stuff like that."
This was pretty much the gist of the communication between the
church in charge of the schools and the Federal Government.

If you look at further correspondence, he adds, you will find
more specifics about schooling and how it was aimed at system-
atically erasing the culture and language from native children's
lives all together:

> this guy named Pratt,[12] his motto was for all of Indian schools, "kill
> the Indian, save the man", that was his motto, and they beat the hell
> out of us and knocked the language and spirituality out of us, so these
> things happened, and a lot of people don't think these are atrocities.
> But I lived through that, I actually was in a school like that.

He continues:

> and you know what? When they put children (in a place like that)
> and they are very strict with them, they build a person that resents
> authority. And you know what? Even though we got beat up, we
> did things that they didn't even find out about. We snuck out of
> those places at night and took off and came back at four in the
> morning and went to the school.

Doug recalls that in those schools that were more like penal
institutions, "we were frightened, we were small kids". As small

kids, they could only resist so much: "They were too big, big men, you know."

LaDonna's experiences were also quite similar: "you see physical abuse, and in the boarding schools it was high sexual abuse, high physical abuse. That's what I know about Christians and priests and stuff. That's the way they are, so a lot of bad things happened in these schools." She remembers one instance when she was in second grade, where "everybody was sleeping and the nuns came and woke us all up in the middle of the night". The day before, two girls from first grade, twins with beautiful long hair, had run away: "And, you know, every time somebody ran away, we laid in our beds and said, 'Oh please, let them get home, let them go, let them get free.' And so they woke us up in the middle of the night the next day and took us all down the basement." There they saw their friends, who had been caught and brought back to the boarding school:

> I remember they sat them [down] and they made us all stand around and they sat the two girls in the middle, in the chairs, and told us what would happen to us if we ran away. And they shaved their heads bald. And I remember for Indian people that's really hard, it's really hard, the only time you cut your hair is when somebody dies. And so, we are in second grade, and you watch this happen. It changes everything.

The nights were the worst, she says:

> at night when you laid in your bed all you would hear is people crying and crying and crying, and what happens to that whole process is a child thinks like a child. "So, why didn't my parents

come get me, why aren't they saving me?" "Why aren't they helping me?" In the meantime, the parents are forbidden to come, forbidden to go there, and so there is disconnect.

The boarding school era is one dark period that to this day
haunts not only those who had to live through it, but also the
youth you grew up listening to the experiences of their elders.
What LaDonna is talking about when she says that an inevitable
disconnect forms in a child's psyche towards his or her family
when subjected to this kind of treatment is absolutely correct.
The Native American culture is one in which children are constantly surrounded by family members, protected, loved. This is
where the strength lies in a society, as Julie back at CRYP tells
us: the family support mechanism. This is a mechanism that runs
strong and was therefore perceived as a big threat by the Federal Government in the nineteenth and early-twentieth centuries,
with its mission to destroy "Indianism" and thus complete the
process of assimilation.

Hyde also states that one way in which assimilation was
enforced initially was through holding up the tribes in reservations, and immediately afterwards targeting the chiefs of tribes,
trying to strip them of any authority, and thus breaking the tribal
structure. The next move was to take the children and break up
the family unit. The children would, in turn, be broken until they
embodied the "ways of the white men", in order to create natural allies for the US government in future – something the school
system managed to achieve to a certain degree: "Some of the boys
came back years later, turned into imitation whites, and most of
them were unhappy. Some died off there in the white men's land
and were never seen again."[13]

This was in fact the original idea behind the founding of a schooling system that was brutal, merciless and unforgiving towards children. Hyde points out that after Carlisle was founded and several other institutions potentially followed in its footsteps, physical abuse in the schools reached such heights that "a bill was introduced into Congress to put a stop to beatings in Indian schools".[14] However, the white lobby – eager to break the Indian – was determined: "They knew that he[15] had men and women on his payroll under the euphemistic designation of disciplinarians, whose main duty was to thump recalcitrant Indian boys and girls into submission." Captain Richard Henry Pratt fought the proposed bill in Washington, and he won. As Hyde writes, "it required another twenty-five years for the government to advance to the point where it could run an Indian school without including thugs on the staff whose duty it was to beat the pupils".[16]

So, why would anyone enrol their children into such a system? In the beginning, it was through subtle coercion. When Carlisle was first founded in 1879, Hyde tells us that it was "a pet project of the Indian Office, and was under the special patronage of Carl Schurz, secretary of the interior".[17] It was an experiment of sorts. A group of whites, interested in what they thought was "Indian welfare", had convinced themselves that "education could solve the Indian problem in just a few years if Indian children were removed from the evil influences of family and tribal relationships and secluded in big government boarding schools, far from the reservations".[18]

Captain Pratt, assigned by the secretary of the interior to the Carlisle School for Indians, was charged with recruiting students for the boarding school. When local resistance ran high among tribesmen not willing to give up their children to an unknown fate, the missionaries at the agencies approached powerful chiefs and talked them into giving up their children as an example, so the rest of their tribesmen would follow suit. Thus, Pratt managed to round up eighty-four pupils from Rosebud and Pine Ridge Agencies, his first flock of students, and took them to Pennsylvania.

Luther Standing Bear was one of the first students taken on a train to Carlisle. His experience of that journey would later be shared in his book *Land of the Spotted Eagle*. Thinking he was being taken away to die at the hands of the white man, this brave young man of eleven years old , rode his pony to the Missouri River, where he would part with his parents, and was put on a boat for the first leg of their journey. "Some of the children changed their minds and were unable to go on the boat, but for many who did go, it was a final parting."[19] Then came the train ride, which cut through terrain that now was inhabited by white settlers. Their travels in and out of train stations along the way were perceived by the local whites as an extravaganza:

> Whenever our train stopped at the railway stations, it was met by great numbers of white people who came to gaze upon the little Indian "savages". The shy little ones sat quietly at the car windows looking at the people who swarmed on the platform. Some of the children wrapped themselves in their blankets, covering all but their eyes.[20]

This circus continued all the way to Pennsylvania, with white spectators mocking and whooping at the children every time their train stopped at a station.

Upon arrival in Carlisle, they were immediately given Christian names, their hair was cut short and they were dressed like white children. When the tribal chiefs visited the school some months later, naturally, all hell broke loose. Chief Spotted Tail threatened to take his children back with him. Instead of learning to read, write and be granted higher education, he said, they were being taught common traits, broken in as farmers, common working men, carpenters and bricklayers. The chiefs accompanying Spotted Tail also regretted ever having subjected their children to such lows. They tried to take their children back as well, but the die had been cast. Soon they would realise there was no turning back. Hyde tells us that the white decision-makers would ultimately realise that they:

> now had to abandon their attitude that the Indian parents longed to send their children to school, and presently a system of compulsion was devised, and every Indian agent became a professional kidnapper who sent his Indian police out to ambush and drag in weeping Indian boys and girls, to be sent off under guard to one of the big government schools.[21]

"My grandma said they took her at five years old and sent her to a boarding school in California, Riverside," LaDonna tells us. "They came and told her that her parents were dead. So she went on with her life, and when she was eighteen they put her on the bus, and sent her back to the reservation, where she never lived since she was a little child." So, there she was:

> standing in the street with a suitcase and no place to go and not know anybody. And the agent here took her and let her stay in a garage. And then she started cleaning house for him, and watching his children. And he came in one day and he said, "Alice, I

have news, your mother and father is still alive, they live down by Mobridge, would you like to go see them?" She was like, "What? Why didn't they come pick me up?", and so she always had this, really, anger against her parents, constantly because they didn't come rescue her. Logically they could not. They were not allowed.

"So, we came out of there and we went to the public schools, we come out of there and we were hardcore," says Doug. "We fought, cos in there we couldn't get along, so if you got in a fight, people gather around you and you fight, they don't stop it. The other kids won't stop it so you went to it." Forcibly taken from a loving environment where they were free, the children were instead placed in a hostile environment where the only way they could survive was by hurting others. "I tell this to people, you know, and [they say] "Oh, it couldn't be that bad". Oh, boy, books have been written by Native Americans about this stuff, you know."

Back in 1933, Luther Standing Bear also wrote about the changes that they were faced with in these boarding schools; with no one to protect them, they were left with no choice but to fight for survival. Not all had the courage or the strength of LaDonna and Doug. So, faced with stark changes to their lifestyles, along with cruelty and loneliness, "in three years, nearly one-half of the children from the Plains were dead and through with all earthly schools. In the graveyard at Carlisle most of the graves are those of the little ones."[22]

These harrowing experiences that still haunt the native communities found a new platform, where they could finally be talked about, in Standing Rock. The truth has an incorrigible way of coming out. As Bobbi Jean mentioned earlier, talking about trauma is one way to help a person heal. Before Standing Rock, she says, the generational trauma was a taboo of sorts: "[I] was kind of taught to, like, I wasn't [supposed] to say anything, to be quiet, to not talk about anything that we go through." Having found her voice through the movement, which "really made me open, open up my own heart and mind to sharing my story with people, or even speaking about it," Bobbi thinks she has taken a big step in terms of her own healing:

> because I do talk about what happened, and I do talk about what happened to my grandmothers and my grandpas and my uncles and my aunties, my mom or dad, my siblings, everybody. I think a lot of it, not just my family, but as a community and probably as a tribe as well, as just like the transition probably from living in tipis to where we are now today, and everything that happened in between. That was a lot of trauma, and I really do believe all that goes back to the boarding schools, when they were trying to civilise us or whatever.

Tammy also believes that the historical trauma that is tearing up Native American society even to this day, if addressed properly, can possibly be healed: "You know, this holistic, compassionate value system that we have, I think [it] definitely slowed down our ability to overcome this trauma," she says. However, today she believes they are in a different state as a society, "where we are able to look at it differently with different eyes and be able to deal with that history a little bit differently. And we are also in a time, you know, that we are able to practice our culture and our identity, and at a time where we were losing that at such a point that people are just very motivated to keep it." She pauses, before adding, "you know, the freedom of religion act, what, 1976? That's when we were finally able to be Indian." She laughs, "that's when the government said, 'It's OK, be Indian now, we're not mad, we're not trying to kill the Indian anymore, you can be Indian now'. 1976, you know!"

Assimilation versus citizenship

The American Indian Religious Freedom Act of 1978[23] that Tammy is referring to is in fact the culmination of a series of bills and acts, including the Citizenship Act of 1924. However, an even earlier mention of native peoples' ascension to US citizenship was made in the ominous Dawes Act (also called the General Allotment or the Dawes Severalty Act) back in 1887, a precursor to the Sioux Bill of 1889. Ardently sponsored in Congress by Massachusetts Senator Henry L. Dawes, the Act promoted individual land ownership of tribesmen. Once passed, Congress would issue 160 acres to each household within a given reservation, and 80 acres to each unmarried adult, with the requirement that the assignees would man their land for at least twenty-five years. Also, per Section 5 of the Act, the United States would be the sole buyer of tribal land, with its Secretary of the Interior acting as negotiator.

The Dawes Act aimed to kill several birds with one stone: through individual ownership, the tribesmen would be introduced to one of the main principles of capitalism; by becoming sedentary farmers, in twenty-five years their assimilation into white society would be complete; and, thanks to a final amendment written into the Act that helped it pass through Congress smoothly, their lands not relegated to individual allotments would be put up for public sale.

The passage on citizenship penned into the Dawes Act, which passed in February 1887, read:

> And every Indian born within the territorial limits of the United States to whom allotments shall have been made under the provisions of this act, or under any law or treaty, and every Indian born within the territorial limits of the United States who has voluntarily taken up, within said limits, his residence separate and apart from any tribe of Indians therein, and has adopted the habits of civilized life, is hereby declared to be a citizen of the United States, and is entitled to all the rights, privileges, and immunities of such citizens, whether said Indian has been or not, by birth or otherwise, a member of any tribe of Indians within the territorial limits of the United States without in any manner affecting the right of any such Indian to tribal or other property.[24]

The "civilized life" referred to in this passage is, unsurprisingly, a life dictated by the norms of white, Christian society. The last section, which mentions tribal membership "through birth or otherwise", would, in a few decades, help dust off and put into effect the archaic and controversial blood quantum laws, written by the British into the charter of the Colony of Virginia in the early-eighteenth century.

The General Allotment Act passed and was eagerly followed with the Sioux Bill in 1889. By the time the land commission of 1889 came knocking on the Sioux's door, the commission members found that even the mere mention of individual land ownership earned much resistance from tribesmen. Older tribal chiefs, who had once fought against the Federal Government and later witnessed the signing and aftermath of the treaties with them, took this "mere mention" as an attempt by Washington to once again break tribal unity while avoiding its responsibilities as cited in these treaties once and for all. They suspected that this was in fact another way for the Federal Government to acquire more of their land by breaking it up to individual lots. They couldn't comprehend why they should be forced to pay taxes to any government for land that rightfully belonged to them.[25]

Hyde cites Oglala Chief American Horse, who acted as the spokesperson for his tribe during the meetings held at these agencies, accurately prophesying that the commission would take "half of the Sioux land today, and tomorrow the tax man would come and tie strings to every bit of the land the Sioux had left. Then the Sioux would have no money to pay the tax man, and he would pull on the strings and drag all the land right out from under the Sioux."[26] In other words, the Sioux Chief understood the solemn repercussions of individual land ownership, and the risk that it could potentially lead to full citizenship, with his tribesmen then being forced to support the government through taxes as opposed to the other way around.

The Federal Government, however, largely influenced by land speculators – including those within its ranks – believed that individual land ownership and through it citizenship being granted to Native Americans would correct a glitch in the system. Washington could then deal with the tribesmen one-on-one to acquire more land, removing the Tribal Council from negotiations. In addition, by granting the rights of a US citizen to an indigenous person, the government would be absorbing that person into American society. *This* – according to many of the Sioux Chiefs and tribesmen – was assimilation complete.

History would prove American Horse and those who staunchly opposed the 1889 land commission right. The effects of the General Allotment Act were devastating. The living conditions in agencies sharply deteriorated, with tribesmen being pushed further into poverty, ripped from their reservation and communal life, and forced into the habits of a white capitalist society, with its vicious cycle of incurring debts and trying to find a means of paying them off.

Four years after the 1924 Indian Citizenship Act, an 872-page detailed survey, authorised by Congress to look into the living conditions of Native Americans in shrinking reservations, would uncover the dimensions of this devastation. Backed up by meticulous field research, *The Problem of Indian Administration* (commonly known as the Meriam Report) is still one of the most detailed documentations of conditions at the reservations in the first half of the twentieth century. That said, by putting the blame for these harrowing conditions on the lack of adjustment of Native Americans "to the economic and social system of the dominant white civilization",[27] this document is living proof that even a study as carefully conducted and lavishly sponsored as the Meriam Report can fail to put the blame, and in this case the responsibility as well, where it truly belongs.

This survey, highlighting the sale and lease of individual plots of land by tribesmen desperate to support themselves and their families, would in turn act as a bitter reminder of the well-founded concerns of the tribal chiefs during the land commission in 1889. Recognising that the Dawes Act had become an absolute train wreck, the surveyors were now telling Congress that it was important, if not vital, to put restrictions on further sale of tribal lands. Calling on the "Friends of the Indians" – the powerful white lobby in Washington that decided what was "good" for the Native Americans – the due section of the report read: "True friends of the Indians should urge retention of restrictions until the Indian is economically on its feet and able to support himself by his own efforts according to a minimum standard of health and decency in the presence of white civilization."[28]

Sociologists Charles Gallagher and Cameron Lippard, editors of an encyclopaedia of race and racism in America, put into perspective the degree of damage caused by the Dawes Act, which became visible soon after the issuance of the survey:

> The Indian population had actually decreased since the passage of the 1887 Indian Allotment Act. There were more landless Indians than before; Indian trust lands had decreased in value; family income was as low as $48 per year on some reservations; the annual death rate had increased; and the Indian land base had shrunk from 137 million acres to a mere 47 million.[29]

The tribal land base had eroded. The native population was destitute. Hunger was eminent if not omnipresent. Dangerous communicable diseases such as trachoma were rampant. Infant mortality was high. What the chiefs had warned would happen if tribal lands were opened up to individual ownership was now a depressing reality: the reservation lands continued to melt away while the tribesmen desperately tried to stay above the poverty line.

BOX 4. Proving identity: blood quantum (or the Indian Blood Laws)
Blood quantum, worked into the final section of the *Indian Reorganization Act* (also known as the *Howard-Wheeler Act*) on 18 June 1934, would define the preconditions necessary

to ensure tribal membership and through it privileges such as claim on tribal land and a share in tribal revenues. The Act had in fact been put into effect to stop the damage the Dawes Act had inflicted on native societies. It aimed to once again redefine the status of land belonging to the native communities, while setting the ground rules for tribal organisation. Through this Act, the practice of individual ownership of tribal land as granted in the Dawes Act would be brought to an end; the term "Indian" would be redefined as a member of any tribe and their descendants recognised by the Federal Government (residing in reservations as of the date the Act passed in Congress); and this term would expand to include "persons of one-half or more Indian blood".

The reintroduction of blood quantum through the Indian Reorganization Act would, over time, split native societies by leaving out those who couldn't prove they had the minimum amount of necessary of "Indianness" in their blood. Tribe members whose "Indian blood" had been reduced through intermarriages – even intertribal marriages – and their offspring, carrying a below-the-minimum requirement amount of "Indian" blood, would be left out, and left with few options other than moving into urban centres and trying to etch out a living in the "white world". This meant double discrimination, first within their own tribe, and soon afterwards in the predominantly white cosmopolitan cities of the United States.

Fast forward to today, and blood quantum is still enforced by certain tribes, whereas others such as the Cherokee Nation declare that it has no blood quantum requirements for tribal membership. However, the discussion continues as to whether it is legal documentation of a person's blood lineage that proves their native identity, or whether it is their way of life, their customs and beliefs, and to what extent those practices take over their lives that determine how "Indian" they are. The curious case of Navajo singer and sound performer Radmilla Cody's identity is an example of the dimensions of the controversy. Born to a Navajo mother and an African-American father, Cody is, from a colonial perspective, a mixed-blood. However, her biracial status is in effect nulled by the fact that she chooses to live a Navajo life.

Cody was the forty-sixth Miss Navajo of the Navajo Nation between 1997 and 1998. This contest, although bearing similarities to its white versions, is no simple beauty pageant, but rather an arduous competition in which contestants need to do everything that is required of a Navajo woman, from gutting sheep to traditional singing and dancing.[30] To this day, among the Navajo she is both revered as a representative of their tribe and denounced for not being a full-blood. Ethnomusicologist Kristina Jacobsen-Bia believes that the resistance to accepting Cody's identity as Navajo "tie[s] crucially into issues of tribal citizenship in Native North America in the era of casinos, where the affective and political stakes of belonging have been dramatically raised, and citizenship and enrolment have come to signify more rigid demarcations between who belongs and who does not".[31]

However, while casino shares and the other tangible benefits of holding a *Certificate of Degree of Indian Blood* card may seem to be at the controversial core of this complicated process of documentation, sociologist Eva Marie Garroutte argues that there is more to it than pure economics. In her book *Real Indians*, while painstakingly elaborating on the nature, complicated history and bureaucracy curtailing tribe members' access to their native identity in the United States, Garroutte, through examples, demonstrates that the real risk behind blood quantum is that it may run native societies into extinction. While "tribes have the exclusive right to create their own legal definitions of identity and to do so in any way they choose", the differences in tribal selection procedures – such as the matriarchal lineage sought by some versus the patriarchal lineage sought by others – in the case of intertribal marriages may produce "legally non-Indian children when the two tribes reckon descent differently. In such cases, legal criteria can tear apart families by pushing certain members off the reservation while allowing others to stay."[32]

To further illustrate this, Garroutte arms us with an example from the matrilineal Onondaga.[33] In 1974, with a growing number of non-natives moving into the Onondaga reservation, and the Tribal Council fearing "that the Federal Government might consequently dissolve the reservation", an order was issued by the council for all non-citizens, including non-citizen spouses, who, Garroutte tells us, were mostly women and the children borne by them to Onondaga men, "to leave the reservation or face ejection". The male citizens were allowed to stay, "of course, but only if they chose to live apart from their wives and mixed-race children". Although most who were affected by the ruling left peacefully, Garroutte writes that others were "forcibly removed. One family burned down its home before leaving."[34]

Similar traumatic examples abound when one starts digging into the different memories of tribesmen who have had to constantly prove their native identity. While, from a certain perspective, legal definitions and proof of racial identity may ease dealings with the Federal Government, others believe that they create confusion over personal identity, that sense of belonging, with the question of who is a "real Indian" and the burden of proof constantly lying on the shoulders of native descendants. On this precise matter, Garroutte quotes one of her interviewees, recalling the words of his adopted grandmother: "Unless a person knows their language, and they know the songs and they know their *culture*, they can have all the pieces of paper in the world and still not be Native American. Because it [identity] is not just a legal document; it's a way of *life*, it's a way of *thinking*, a way of *living*, a way of worship that you can't instil on someone with a notarized legal document."[35]

Trauma that transcends time

Historical trauma, when it goes unaddressed, may travel through time, through generations in fact. Studies in the fields of psychology, psychiatry and genetics are trying to explain through epigenetics, or the reversible effects of environmental factors on reshaping our DNA, whether or not transgenerational trauma, or trauma coded into our genes over generations, is a reality.

Dr Çaghan Kızıl, group leader at the German Center of Neurodegenerative Diseases, is a genetics expert working on this subject. Observing laboratory animals, he believes, may help us to understand the genetic undertones at the root of conditions such as post-traumatic stress disorder (PTSD) in youth born into families who have survived traumatic episodes such as genocide. He offers one example of a study done on laboratory fish, which, having been bred in captivity for generations, and despite never having seen a predator, "code" certain events as dangerous using "a reservoir of neural computation". "They get scared and flee when a picture or a life-size cut-out of a fisherman is put near their pond," he explains. This is just one of the many studies being done on laboratory animals that lead geneticists to believe "that this information, which has been coded into their DNA and has been dormant through several generations, [will] all of a sudden become active, and information [will] become available to help the fish flee to safety."

The instinctive fear coded into the DNA of fish, helping them to survive, is a natural part of evolution. Pain, anger and fear, when coded into the DNA of human beings through traumatic experiences such as ethnic cleansing, massacres, forced migrations or simply unaddressed grievances, and when fostered in an environment immersed in poverty, discrimination, alcoholism, substance abuse, violence and crime, can translate into chronic depression and suicidal tendencies.

A recent article by psychiatrist Amy Bombay of the University of Ottawa, psychologist Kimberly Matheson and neuroscientist Hymie Anisman, both of Carleton University, aims to address the psychological dimension of historical trauma, starting with the traumatic conditions at the Indian residential schools in Canada and carrying on through generations of native communities.[36] The authors start by stating that, despite several prior traumatic experiences due to colonialism, the nineteenth century saw Canada creating government policies geared towards assimilating native communities, on whom the white elites looked down as savages. The Indian residential school (IRS) system was put forward as an answer to this overarching government policy of full-blown assimilation, and children as young as three years old were forced by law to attend these schools, leaving behind the life they knew, their families and their communities. The schools were designed to erase any trace of native culture from them, literally to the point of death. Significant number of mortalities were recorded within the system, along with several children who were reported "missing". The article mentions that many children forced to go through the IRS system were victims of neglect as well as chronic mental, physical and sexual abuse. While teaching the children to be "ashamed of their languages, cultural beliefs and traditions", these schools were "largely ineffective at providing proper or even adequate education". For the survivors and their offspring, these traumatic experiences later manifested themselves as a cycle of domestic, sexual and substance abuse, depression and suicidal tendencies.[37] Based on recent data, the article cites that rates of suicide, drug addiction and learning difficulties at school were higher (at times double) for native children and adults who had at least one family member subjected to IRSs than for others who had no family members subjected to the system. Survivors of IRSs inadvertently transferred the trauma they went through to their offspring, "through social disadvantages, and directly by altering parenting behaviours".[38] For example, having parents who were victims of sexual abuse in an IRS in turn increased the risk that a child would also be victimised in a domestic setting, and demonstrate a tendency not to report his or her experience of abuse. Since "a large proportion of Aboriginal children from across Canada were forced to attend IRSs, which intentionally sought to assimilate Aboriginal peoples and destroy their culture",[39] this, over time, played the cardinal role in destroying native society.

As the authors also stress, sexual abuse does not happen in a vacuum. It often exists alongside other forms of physical or psychological abuse and, aided by neglect, leads to dysfunctional families who lack the strength to defend their young. However, according to Bombay and her colleagues, this vicious cycle the child finds themselves in may start quite early: the seeds of it may even be sown during pregnancy. "Behavioural and biological responses to later stressors are exaggerated," the article explains, adding that negative experiences the baby is subjected to during both the prenatal phase and within his or her first few months of being born are the culprits behind later negative behaviours, with the outcomes potentially being similar to those experienced by the offspring of Holocaust survivors.[40]

As epigenetics is known to be a reversible phenomenon, Tammy seems to have found one way of dealing with this inherited trauma. Talking about back when she started work at CRYP, she says: "I think it's interesting, because I wanted to become a social worker, because I wanted to help people not have to die from things they have no control over ... You know the term of cycle-breakers? I say that to my kids all the time." When they get naughty and attempt to do something bad, she tells them, "Well, we are not gonna do that baby, we are a family of cycle-breakers!" She is right: unless the cycle of abuse is broken, society must brace itself for further loss of their young people to suicide.

Returning to the 2005 Senate Committee on Indian Affairs session on suicide among American Indian youths, and once again lending an ear to Dr Stone's testimony, we hear him speak of a twenty-one-year-old male, a drug addict, who jumped off a bridge. He had never previously sought help from the mental health centre at his reservation, fearing social stigma; however, he had talked about his suicidal intentions with his family members. Substance abuse, depression and fiscal problems may have intensified the young man's decision to stop his car on the bridge on that day, step out and dive into the river beneath, says Stone, adding: "We do not know if it was a genuine attempt to kill himself or if he was simply acting out of a substance abuse-induced haze." That hardly matters. Three days after this suicide, a second male tribe member, a relative of the first victim, hung himself. This second suicide took place in Canada, and Dr Stone testifies that the victim acted out with full knowledge of the first one, and that a lack of professional services or community outreach paved the way for this second death: "When he found out about the first suicide of his relative, he said he had found a way out of his pain."

These two deaths, apparently interconnected, deeply affected the community. People expressed fear, grief and helplessness. Dr Stone tells the Committee that a week after the second suicide there were four other suicide attempts: a seventeen-year-old girl, who was a friend of the first victim; another seventeen-year-old boy, who tried to kill himself by ramming into the wall at his jail cell and breaking his neck; a twelve-year-old boy, who after a first botched attempt confessed to Dr Stone that he wanted to jump off the same bridge as the first suicide victim; and a nine-year-old boy, who climbed a tree, contemplating jumping, and was talked down by Dr Stone and the local police.

During the course of the proceedings, Senator Gordon Smith asks Dr Richard Carmona, a surgeon general called in for his expertise, about any prior research he may have come across on suicide among the native population: "In asking this question, I think I know the answer, because I do not think records were kept," he asserts, before inquiring whether any prior research or "historical evidence" of suicide among native communities prior to the westward expansion of white settlers exists.

Dr Carmona's answer is an unfortunate "No", but in reality there *are* records. They do not exist as statistics per say, but diligent research into old texts reveals suicide was sought as a last option in many instances by native communities.

One such extensive reference is within E. T. Denig's long-form article from the nineteenth century. He not only gives suicide its own sub-heading but leaves us with a detailed record of occurrences and what it means for the Assiniboin:

> Widows do not burn themselves on the funeral pile on the decease of their husbands, but frequently hang themselves for that loss, revenge, or for the loss of their children. Three suicides of this kind have been committed within the last few months in this neighborhood among the Assiniboin, one for revenge, the other two for the loss of their children. The first was the favourite wife of a camp soldier, who being scolded and accused of crime by the eldest wife, after telling her purpose, left the lodge, in the absence of her husband, and disappeared. Although search was made, yet a week elapsed before she was discovered hanging to the limb of a tree. She had climbed the tree, tied the cord to the limb, and descending, hooked on the noose standing on the ground, suspending her body by drawing up her legs. She hung so low that her knees nearly touched the ground and she could have risen to her feet at any time during the operation.
>
> Another woman had her son (a young man) killed by the Black-feet, and immediately afterwards another of her children died from disease. Several persons were appointed to watch the mother, suspecting her intentions; but they all fell asleep and she hung herself

at the door of the lodge, between two dog travailles set on end. She was a tall woman and could only produce strangulation by swinging herself off the ground from her feet. She did it, however, and the body was brought to the fort for interment.

The third was a still more unfortunate case. The child of this woman had been sick some time and was expected to die. On the night in question it fell into a swoon and was to all appearance dead. No person being present the mother in the derangement of the moment went out and hung herself. The child recovered, but the mother was dead.

Every year in this way the women hang themselves, sometimes for the loss of their husbands, but more frequently on account of the death of their children, or for revenge. Suicides are also common among the men. They generally use the gun to produce death.[41]

Without a true understanding of the significance of suicide among native communities, no immediate ailment can be offered. In 2005, during her testimony before the Committee, Julie stated that in 2002 and 2003 they had lost seventeen young people to suicide in Cheyenne River alone: "In a community as small as ours, it is all very personal because they are our neighbours, our relatives. We know their mothers, their fathers, their grandmas and their grandpas. They are my nieces and my nephews." In the present day at CRYP, referring to the youth who grow up in reservations, she tells us, "I think that there is something that is always absent. I think that you kind of know it, maybe you don't acknowledge it, but I think you always know it if there is something missing. If you weren't raised with your language and your culture and your cere-monies and all that sort of stuff," she explains, there is always a void in you that continuously yearns to be filled by belonging:

I can speak for myself, you know, when I would hear people talking about going to ceremony, or going to Sun Dances, and you
know it being a little foreign to me, I know what they are back then
but I have not actually been a part of it, so I think that you kind
of wonder, "What's that about? Is there a secret?" And then you
crave it, because other people have it.

What Julie is talking about is similar to what Tammy was saying with regard to the emptiness that exists inside a person whose
identity has been stolen. To address this void, Julie suggests that
families need to take action early on, and introduce their kids to
the native way of life, "but that doesn't always happen. It doesn't
always happen because you have a lot of families that are hurting."
Having worked with kids at CRYP since 1988, Julie knows
what she is talking about. Back in 2005, when Dr Stone mentioned the accumulative grievances that members of native tribes
had experienced over the course of their lives, both prior to but
mostly after being confined to reservations, Julie, recognising this
fact, pointed out that reservation life could also be a way out of
this deadlock:

We all know the history of the reservation, when we were told what
to wear, what to eat, how to dress, how to think, and even how and
when to pray. Although that history is tragic, it is that reservation
system that may now be our salvation, because we are remotely
located and come from close, small, close-knit communities.

With teenage suicides a major cause for concern in the community and among young people living on reservations around the
time these testimonies were being collected in Washington DC,

CYRP was trying to wind back the clock. As a community-driven, grassroots initiative, the project gave hope to young people where little existed. Listening to their needs, and using their own resources, the community started to build the youth centre on the reservation, creating a safe space in which the youth could flourish. More than a decade prior, in front of the Committee, Julie had said she believed such a centre alone could give them "what they need most, which is hope. Now, when they look on the horizon of Cheyenne River, they see a teen centre, which again represents hope."

Fast forward to 2017, which finds us sitting inside the Centre, a dream realised, and talking about what has changed for youth on reservations today. Julie continues to stress that without addressing the root causes of "the problems", no advancement can be made. She believes the solution lies in making use of the strong familial networks that still exists in native communities: "I think that we have really strong family systems," she says, "we have our spiritual leaders, we have our medicine men, we have our traditional ways of doing things and I think what people are realising is that going back to those old ways is really gonna be a big part of finding and healing ourselves." Reflecting on her personal experience of finding her Lakota roots, she adds: "I wasn't raised in that sort of environment, so, me too, I'm trying to find my way back."

In light of these suicides, tormenting native communities for generations, Standing Rock symbolised a hope that things might finally be beginning to change for the better. With it, there came a renewed purpose and understanding that nothing, and especially not life, needs to remain in a stalemate. The communal protests provided vast opportunities for native communities to come together; talk about their past experiences; have their own people and outsiders listen to them; and, through sharing, maybe even begin to heal themselves.

When asked how she thinks the events at Standing Rock Sioux Reservation have affected the young people living in reservations, Tammy explains:

> One of the things that happens to a lot of people is that when people don't listen to you, then you feel you lose that sense of a voice. And eventually it tears you down too much that you lack the confidence to use your voice. You know, you lose the courage to use it. Because what's the point? You know nobody is listening, it doesn't matter.

She believes that through Standing Rock native young people have not only regained their voice but also realised that, "if I believe in something, if I care about something, if something is not what it should be; if we are being hurt, if we are being oppressed, if we're being ignored, we can keep talking till somebody listens, we can keep voicing our opinion about this till somebody listens, and I think that's especially powerful".

And that voice regained may eventually succeed in laying to rest the grievances that have been haunting the tribesmen for over 150 years, almost ever since the Lakota and Cheyenne victory at the Battle of Little Big Horn.

THREE | The black snake

Have we not for years had before our eyes a sample of their designs, and are they not sufficient harbingers of their future determinations? Will we not soon be driven from our respective countries and the graves of our ancestors? Will not the bones of our dead be plowed up, and their graves be turned into fields? Shall we calmly wait until they become so numerous that we will no longer be able to resist oppression? Will we wait to be destroyed in our turn, without making an effort worthy of our race? Shall we give up our homes, our country, bequeathed to us by the Great Spirit, the graves of our dead, and everything that is dear and sacred to us, without a struggle? I know you will cry with me: Never! Never!
(Tecumseh, Shawnee Chief, addressing the Choctaw and Chickasaw)

Tuncosila, Wakan Tanka, save me and give me all my wild game animals. Bring them near me, so that my people may have plenty to eat this winter. Let good men on Earth have more power, so that all nations may be strong and successful. Let them be of good heart, so that all Sioux people may get along well and be happy. If you do this for me, I will perform the sun-gazing dance two days, two nights, and give you a whole buffalo.
(Hunkpapa Chief Sitting Bull's vow before his Sundance in 1876)[1]

We have a rule, rule number one: there is no one way, but our ways are thousand years old. (LaDonna Tamakawastewin Allard)

People of the Plains

The Great Plains in the Dakotas is a land mass that expands majestically towards the horizon, for miles yielding not a living soul except the occasional herd of bison or family of bucks. Aside from the road signs telling you that you have exited Cheyenne River or entered Standing Rock Reservation, the view is one vast continuum. However, if you look closely, you will notice that the otherwise continuous landscape in the reservations is in fact partitioned into lots, with light fences drawn around individual allotments. These partitions act as reminders of the white idea of "owning" land that has been imposed on the native communities, along with the unavoidable and desperate execution of this idea by tribesmen through land sales and leases to white ranchers over the centuries following the Dawes Act of 1887.

"Back in the day, all these plains belonged to the Lakota," reminisce the people of the present-day reservations scattered around the Great Plains. The Lakota Sioux, boasting an ancestral lineage of legendary chiefs and warriors such as Sitting Bull and Crazy Horse, were free roamers, buffalo hunters, and territorial enemies of the Crows and Arikara, against whom they often went on the warpath. Much like other tribes in the Plains, they were also successful raiders. Back then, these raids were a show of courage and a traditional way of claiming territory as one's own. According to historical geographer David Wishart, some of this raiding activity "involved revenge, perhaps a retaliation to an enemy's previous attack, but the prime motivation by 1800 was profit, especially in the form of horses". As the tribes sported a communal social structure, upon the war party's return to the village, the spoils from their successful day's raiding "might be given as gifts to the village chief or to the priest who, as representative of the war bundle, had sanctioned the raid". Despite the hereditary nature of tribal leadership in native societies, displays of courage such as attending a raid, or of generosity such as giving away the spoils, were the means by which a warrior could rise through social ranks.[2]

E. T. Denig also writes extensively about the warriors of the Crow Nation, depicting them as successful raiders. He mentions that these raids, with the importance of horse ownership translating into personal wealth within the tribe, made the Crows "perhaps the richest nation in horses of any residing east of the Rocky Mountains. It is not uncommon for a single family to be the owner of 100 of these animals. Most middle-aged men have from 30 to 60. An individual is said to be poor when he does not possess at least 20."

So, before the white man set his mind on settling in these vast tracts of land, raids on herds of horses constituted a large portion of what Denig calls "continual war" between tribes such as the Crow and Blackfeet Nations, where "scarcely a week passes but large numbers are swept off by the war parties on both sides". Wars lost called for revenge, and throughout these clashes, in a single hunting season, Denig writes that "several hundred animals in this way change owners. A great portion of the time of each nation is occupied either in guarding their own horses or in attempts to take those of their enemies."[3]

On the back of such a history, as recently as the nineteenth century the Plains still belonged to the tribes and the tribes alone, with shifting borderlines – the nature of which colonial minds couldn't easily grasp – and often overlapping territories, where tribesmen hunted and moved around. However, with the introduction of European traders, the environment around the Plains' tribes started changing drastically and at a precipitous pace. First, game ran short due to excessive hunting to quench the thirst of the whites, who primarily traded in fur. With a strain on resources and hunger imminent, the movement of tribes began to occur for a single reason: survival. The Dakota, for instance, fierce hunters and warriors, soon started to move down from their northern dwellings and put pressure on the Omaha, Ponca and Pawnee of current-day Nebraska.

Wishart writes about the overlapping tribal territories in eastern Nebraska in the nineteenth century, when the land claims of individual tribes extended well into the boundaries of others. Talking of the Ponca, he tells us that they claimed the land extending from "the White River on the north, to the Platte on the south. The eastern boundary of this claimed homeland ran south from the Missouri near present-day Sioux City to the Platte; the western limit was nebulous, but the Ponca believed that it was beyond the Black Hills."[4] However, the Ponca's claim over such a large expanse of land was disputed by other tribes, which often led to skirmishes between them and the Omaha, Pawnee and Teton Dakota.

The Sioux moved with the buffalo, which was their livelihood. So, it was the annual bison hunts that made these territorial claims more important and, as the fur trade sped up, more violent. Tribes that had hunted only to fill their own needs and in a manner that was sustainable would soon begin to hunt not only for food and hides but for European merchandise as well. These hunts and complex rivalries between tribes and over game would force the Pawnee into contention

with the Comanche, Cheyenne, and Arapahoe on the upper reaches of the Platte and Republican rivers, and the Ponca were often

harassed by the Brulé Dakota along the Niobrara. The Otoe-Mis-
souria periodically clashed with the Kansa and Osage on their hunts,
and, as Lewis and Clark had discovered, the Nebraska Indians often
clashed with each other.[5]

Still, in the early nineteenth century the Dakota fighters had
not yet been entirely forced out of the Great Lakes region by the
populous Ojibwa bands, who had migrated there from the east
coast,[6] and thus had "not fully expanded into the Nebraska Indians' bison range". With these bands not yet in the picture as fully
as they would be in later years, the seasonal hunts were a (relatively) "less hazardous operation than in later years".[7]

In the eighteenth century and well beyond the turn of nineteenth century, bison were still plentiful, with the fur trade still
being relatively small in size. However, time would bring fierce
competition, with large trading companies entering the market to
replace individual traders, demanding more and at lower prices.
The tribes would soon be introduced to capitalist notions such
as lines of credit, and tribesmen would find themselves stuck in a
vicious cycle of trying to pay off debts, the amount and terms of
which were mandated by white traders.

From a European perspective, land, like game, was also in
abundance in the Great Plains, its significance for the native
tribes largely lost on early explorers. The latter believed, possibly due to the overlapping nature of tribal land claims, that the
indigenous people did not hold title to these lands: a misperception that still resonates today. Wishart talks of early explorers
completely missing the esoteric role played by prominent land
features – hills, buttes, caves – in the everyday lives of the Plains
Indians as pilgrimage sites, spots to seek visions or give offerings.

The animals that roamed the landscape, whose power tribes' medicine men sought to heal the sick, were as important to the native population as they were poorly understood by the whites who came their way:

> Lewis and Clark were unable to appreciate this symbiotic relationship with nature. (Perhaps they were exhibiting a degree of wishful thinking, because even in 1804 President Jefferson harbored the idea of transferring eastern Indians into the Great Plains.) They concluded that the Indians of eastern Nebraska had "no idea of an exclusive possession of any country".[8]

This conclusion – an unfortunate mistake at best, or a conventional oversight – was one that would continue to haunt the relationships between tribes and whites. Around the time the US government was getting ready to celebrate its centennial and continue its expansion westward, this very idea – empowered by the Doctrine of Discovery – would guide the Federal Government's dealings with native tribes, both along the warpath and throughout the signing of treaties leading to ominous land cessions.

By the mid-nineteenth century, with more settlers moving west, demands for land had grown. With bison stocks on the decline due to excessive hunting, the fur trade had lost its former glory, and market interest had shifted towards trading land instead. Clashes between the whites and the tribes became commonplace, with settlers keen on driving the natives away and clearing territory for themselves. It was a fight for survival, and there were hardly any winners among those physically fighting it out on the ground. The only people doubling their profits were the rich land speculators and the political elite settled on the east coast.

In the 1860 text *Kitchi-Gami*, German traveller Johann Kohl, who lived among the Ojibwa in the Great Lakes region during the mid-1800s and recorded their customs, writes about a council held between government officials and tribesmen, during which a member of the Ojibwa band stood up and voiced his objection to this unbridled white desire for land in the Americas. Here is an excerpt from his timeless speech, its righteous tone of disapprobation resonating to this day:

> When the white men first came into this country and discovered us, we received them hospitably, and if they were hungry, we fed them, and went hunting for them. At first the white men only asked for furs and skins. I have heard from our old men that they never asked for anything else. These we gave them gladly, and received from them their iron goods, guns, and powder.
>
> But for some years they have been asking land from us. For ten years they have asked from us nothing but land, and ever more land. We give unwillingly the land in which the graves of our fathers rest. But for all that we have given land in our generosity. We knew not that we were giving so much for so little. We did not know that such great treasures of copper were hidden in our land.
>
> The white men have grown rich by the bargain. When I look round me in this assembly, I notice rich golden watch-chains and golden rings on the clothes and fingers of many men; and when I look in the faces of the people who are so richly adorned, I always see that their colour is white, and not red. Among the red men I never see anything of the sort! [T]hey are all so poorly clad! [T]hey are miserably poor![9]

At this point, Kohl tells us the speaker pointed to a group of tribesmen exhibiting signs of extreme poverty to make his case. He then continued:

> We are not only poor, but we have also debts. At least, people say that we have debts. On the former treaty and payment we also paid debts. I fancied then we paid them all. But now the old question is addressed to us. A number of old things are brought against us from an old bag. Where these debts come from, I know not.

Colonialists

The struggle for existence started the moment Christopher Columbus set foot in the Americas and invoked the powers of the fifteenth-century Papal Bulls, which granted explorers the "right" to claim title to non-Christian lands they had "discovered". He and his men, not interested in the richness of the cultures they encountered so much as the land, their eyes set on exploitation, set the pattern for those who came after. The terms used today to reference all native tribes of the Americas – "Indians" or "American Indians" – are a remnant of those days.

To understand the mindset shared by Columbus and his successors – that is, conveniently bundling indigenous tribes into one homogeneous identity – it is important to know that in the fifteenth century a huge chunk of what is now Southeast Asia was also bundled together by colonialists into a single region called the Indies. Today, it is widely believed that Columbus, originally thinking he had landed on the Indies when in fact he had arrived in the Americas, consequently called the people he encountered "Indians", a term that stuck thereafter.

Roger Williams references this in *A Key into the Language of America*, in a curious little aside. The text acts as a sad reminder of the fact that these powerful and independent nations with distinct characteristics could not understand why they were being bundled into one homogeneous mass with a common title: "They have often asked mee [sic], why wee [sic] call them *Indians Natives*, & c. And understanding the reason, they will call themselues [sic] *Indians*, in opposition to *English*, & c."[10]

LaDonna also shares this disbelief. To this arrogance of the colonial mind, with its complete disregard for tribes' cultural diversity, she duly objects:

> we don't really fit into a classification because there is no 'Native American culture'. There are native people with many cultures. Many languages. And we don't understand each other. So in North Dakota we have Cree, Chippewa, Hidathsa, Mandan, Arikara, Lakota, Dakota. Seven tribes. We all don't understand each other's culture, spirituality; our way of life, our cultures are also different from each other, we don't know each other's culture. And we all live in one state.

The decrees issued by the Vatican, which the conquistadors exploited in the New World, would, during the Confederation Period, translate into the idea that the United States automatically held title to the lands it invaded by "right of conquest." In *American Indians and State Law*, historian Deborah Rosen sheds light on this early period, the origins of such a convenient misperception and its evolution into a discovery doctrine: "When it soon became apparent that the country did not have the military or economic wherewithal to act unilaterally with regard to Native peoples, the government modified its stance by acknowledging that the Indians had a right to retain possession and ownership of their lands."[11] Instead of acquiring land *de facto* through "a theoretical and mythical right of conquest", the Federal Government took the route of treaties, and later land commissions, exercising a fierce version of capitalism under which tribes were often left with very little choice but to sign these bilateral agreements.

The United States Congress would soon detail its position with regard to ownership of land in the American Midwest – bordered by Pennsylvania to the east, the Ohio River to the south, the Mississippi River to the west and the Great Lakes to the north – by issuing the Northwest Ordinance of 1787. The last of the three ordinances laying down the basis of governance for the Northwest Territories of the United States, this would also lay the ground rules for any future dealings and potential treaties with Indian tribes:

> The utmost good faith shall always be observed towards the Indians; their lands and property shall never be taken from them without their consent; and in their property, rights and liberty, they never shall be invaded or disturbed, unless in just and lawful wars authorised by Congress; but laws found in justice and humanity shall from time to time be made, for preventing wrongs being done to them, and for preserving peace and friendship with them.[12]

However, as time passed dynamics changed, and those in Washington shifted their view of land ownership to one that suited them best. Coupled with the US Army improving its military capacity, bringing new and more advanced artillery into the equation, dealing with the tribes became less of a concern. As Rosen continues to tell us, when the tribes ceased to become a "military threat and were no longer ceding territory quickly enough to satiate American land hunger, greater ambivalence about treaty relationships with Indian tribes emerged, and some Americans claimed that the past practice of negotiating with tribes was a mere fictional convenience rather than a legal mandate".[13] So, to expedite things, by the 1820s Washington once again dusted off and put back into effect "the right of conquest", which it claimed "gave the United States underlying title to Indian lands".[14]

The Federal Government's return to the old practice of instigating "the right of conquest" over the native tribes and their land would be recorded for posterity in the famous lawsuit *Johnson v. M'Intosh*. This 1823 case was about the purchase of a certain plot of land by Thomas Johnson from the Piankeshaw Tribe in private as well as by William M'Intosh directly from the Federal Government. The Supreme Court would rule the M'Intosh purchase valid, obstructing any further private dealings of land between indigenous and nonindigenous people.

The decision by Chief Justice John Marshall upheld the notion that the United States, despite having declared independence from Britain, inherited its "right of conquest". This read as, unless a tribe could claim full title to a plot of land, which would then require a separate dealing between the tribe and the Federal Government, lands in which tribes could only claim "incomplete" ownership would no longer be considered tribal lands, and thus their ownership automatically transferred to the Federal Government. Either way, the tribes were not free to choose with whom they dealt, should they wish to sell their lands. The US government was the exclusive buyer and, in the absence of competition, would be the party that set the price.

Thus, if we go back to the original theory that Columbus thought he was in the Indies when in fact he had landed in the Americas, and that his original motive was not to encounter new cultures but to exploit the land and its resources in the name of the crown, it is unsurprising that he bundled the indigenous tribes he encountered into one homogeneous group with a single name: Indians, the people of the Indies. This also helps us to visualise the mindset of those who came after him; those who also claimed the land, first for the crown and later for themselves. The indigenous nations never really mattered or had much of a chance. They were the "others", a mere detail standing in the way of the expansion of colonies, to be dealt with at times violently and at other times cunningly – and always at minimum cost.

Land: a most precious commodity

When early colonists arrived in the Americas, intertribal warfare for control of territory among the local peoples was nothing new. With the arrival of white settlers, however, it took on a different form. Now there was a new variable in the equation, and one that could be turned into an ally or an enemy, an opportunity or a threat. Therefore, depending on how the native tribes perceived the colonists, they shaped their positions and relations with them accordingly. Some decided to cooperate with these newcomers, while others, seeing them as invaders, decided to stand up against the intrusion. Some alliances formed out of necessity, but more often than not they were opportunistic, and in most instances they greatly benefited those who had just arrived: so much so that, by the time tribesmen realised the toll these so-called alliances were taking on them and their people, it was already too late.

The gradual removal of tribes from their territories started soon after settlers arrived on the east coast. As cities and towns began springing up, the first tribes to be pushed west or largely disappear were those that bordered the shoreline, such as the Massachuset. They perished from diseases introduced by European colonists. Schlesier reveals "that the overall mortality from the 1616–19 and 1633–39 epidemics in New England, stood at no less than 86 percent of the Indian populations".[15] Today, although a few descendants from that tribe are said to inhabit the greater Boston area, what is mostly left of them is the name of the state.

The Montauk band of the Lenape people inhabiting Long Island shared a similar fate: intertribal warfare coupled with outbreaks of smallpox contracted from Dutch and English colonists, with whom the tribe traded, wiped out a large portion of their population. Near breaking point, on 3 May 1639 the once influential Montaukett chief Wyandanch signed off a portion of the tribe's land to an English settler and former military man, Lion Gardener.[16] This agreement was most likely made in the hope it would offer protection against future attacks from other tribes, primarily the Narragansett, who resided north of the Montauk in what is now Rhode Island. The Narragansett were, at the time, one of the more powerful tribes, harbouring a desire to expand their territory and control a larger part of the fur trade with the colonists. Through this treaty signed with the Montauk, Gardener became the owner of a large island east of Long Island, then called the Isle of Wight, which went down in history as "the earliest English settlement within the present limits of the state of New York".[17]

Gardener penned a text in 1660 that was misplaced, only to be rediscovered more than two decades later and printed by the

Massachusetts Historical Society.[18] *Relation of the Pequot War-res* offers a first-hand account of the "decisive struggle between the first settlers and their Indian neighbours",[19] where the author gives us a glimpse of, from a settler's perspective, what it was like along the tumultuous Connecticut River Valley in early 1600. The manuscript, written in colloquial English, consists of Gardener's detailed observations of the interactions between early colonial settlers and local tribes as well as the effects of trade and the desire to control it. While meticulously describing the lay of the land and individual skirmishes, especially between the Pequots and white settlers, the narrative offers a window into one of the defining periods in the history of the continent, and vital information with regard to the effect settlers had on native populations.

It is also here that we read candid details about Gardener and his men getting involved in small clashes with individual bands of Pequots during their hit-and-run raids on settlers, stealing crops or abducting women, the latter of which would later be rescued by Dutch sailors and returned to the small colony. He recalls: "Canoe wherein 2 maids were that were taken by the Indians whom I redeemed and clothed for the Dutchmen who I sent to fetch them brought them away almost naked from Pequit they putting their own linen jackets to cover their nakedness."[20]

In his manuscript, after detailing this rescue operation, Gardener goes on to complain about the financial cost of the entire ordeal, which he paid for out of his own pocket, and for which he had not yet been thanked, and says that he's not even sure whether or not these events are known to "the Mayor".[21] This prioritisation of self-interest continues to resonate through the Federal Government's dealings with tribes to this day. The native communities, once sovereign nations with boundaries, would soon be coerced into signing treaties that served the best interests of the newly formed Federal Government; yet they continued to be perceived as a burden with which to be dealt, and at unnecessary expense.

As the fur trade heated up, individual traders would not back down from pitting native communities against each other, profiting from their rivalries – a strategy that would also be adhered to by Washington time and again in its later dealings with the tribes. Sometimes these rivalries, escalated by the whites for profit, would even manifest as intratribal rebellions as opposed to intertribal wars, culminating in acts of violence as serious as assassinations of tribal chiefs by their own tribesmen.

Going back to Gardener's manuscript, we read about the early colonists benefiting from shifting alliances defined by distrust and continuous warfare among different tribes; white traders seeking alliances with the Mohegans, and later with the Uncas; and Gardener himself asking the brother of the Chief of Long Island to bring him the heads of all the Pequots as a sign of goodwill as well as the heads of any "Indian[s] that have killed English" if the chief's people wished to trade with him: a deal, Gardener says, the chief of the Montauk did not refuse.[22]

During this early colonial period, as cities and towns along the eastern shore were beginning to take shape, the vast Heartland was left mostly undisturbed, except for the occasional intrusion by an explorer. On the world map, however, North America was divided up between the colonial powers of England, France and Spain. The wars raging on in Europe affected settlers' ownership of land in the Americas, and land purchases such as the great Louisiana Purchase were attached to truces signed between warring nations in a foreign continent across the ocean. The fate of the tribes inhabiting these lands would thus be determined by nations who knew or cared little about them.

Political scientist Michael Rogin, writing about the policies and events culminating in US president Andrew Jackson's Indian Removal Act, tells us exactly this: "Indians inhabited in 1790 almost all the territory west of the original thirteen states. If America were to expand and take possession of the continent, they would have to be dispossessed. Indians had not mattered so much, in the history of Europeans in the English new world, since the colonial settlements. They would never matter so much again."[23]

The Andrew Jackson era is known for American expansion into the west. With cities on the east coast becoming over-crowded, populating the land westward towards the Pacific Ocean would become central to American politics. In his book *A People's History of the United States*, unorthodox historian Howard Zinn details the chronology of events that would culminate in the "Indian Removal" under Jackson, who is a land specula-tor, slaveholder and Indian exterminator in Zinn's narrative as opposed to the "soldier, democrat and man of the people" he is often depicted as in traditional history books.[24]

However, as Wishart highlighted earlier, prior to Jackson's removal of native communities from land the Federal Govern-ment had set aside for expansion were Thomas Jefferson's plans. Back in 1803, the Louisiana Purchase promised more land to the young United States to expand westward, its already-exist-ing inhabitants a mild nuisance that needed to be dealt with. A couple of decades later, during his tenure between 1829 and 1837, Jackson would realise Jefferson's dream. Zinn offers us a chance to look at the flipside of the coin, the noncolonial version of history, in which Andrew Jackson would not only expand the borders of the country but also open up more land to trade.[25] Thus, the Creek and Cherokee would be forced from Georgia, with all tribes in the way of the settlers being "encouraged to settle down on smaller tracts and do farming". The ultimate plan was that they would be "encouraged to trade with whites, to incur debts and then to pay off these debts with tracts of land".[26]

M. P. Rogin provides the numbers for the Jackson era's white expansion:

> Two-thirds of the American population of 3.9 million lived within fifty miles of the [Atlantic] ocean in 1790. In the next half-century 4.5 million Americans crossed the Appalachians, one of the great migrations in world history. The western states contained less than three percent of the U.S. population in 1790, twenty-eight percent in 1830. In two decades the west would become the most populous region of the country.[27]

As for the original inhabitants of the land into which these populations were moving:

> 125,000 Indians lived east of the Mississippi in 1820. Seventy-five percent of these came under government removal programs in the next two decades. By 1844 less than 30,000 Indians remained in the east, mainly in the undeveloped Lake Superior region. Most of the eastern tribes had been relocated west of the Mississippi; the total population of Indians indigenous to the east had declined by one-third.[28]

Indian Removal Act" did what it intended to do and more: it not only cleared the land east of the Mississippi of native people through a largely involuntary exodus, but also paved the way for settlers to set their eyes on more land in the Great Plains. Over time, agencies and later reservations set up by the Federal Government to control tribes in the Heartland did the rest, pushing different native communities together and away from the vast terrains they were accustomed to roaming and hunting in, and forcing them into tight spaces with continuously tightening borders, making them farm, trying to erase their differences through assimilation, throwing them into one homogeneous pool, and ultimately hoping they would either disappear completely or melt into the new country that was being built along a "Trail of Tears".[29]

During expansion at the turn of the eighteenth century, land was the number one commodity as far as white settlers were concerned – one to be grabbed, owned and traded – and nothing would stand in the way of profits. Putting plots of native land up for sale was common practice. As Zinn tells us, in North Carolina even lands belonging to the Chickasaws, who had fought alongside the US Army during the Revolution, were put on sale, despite a treaty having previously been signed that guaranteed their land would go untouched. A young Andrew Jackson, speculating in land, had already made several trips in and out of Nashville in 1795 for land purchases.[30]

Tecumseh, the legendary Shawnee chief and spiritual leader, could foresee his people's future while it was still taking shape. In 1811, he called for a large gathering of tribes. Zinn writes that it was "an Indian gathering of five thousand, on the bank of the Tallapoosa River in Alabama".[31] Having grown up west of the Ohio Valley, where several Shawnee villages – including his own – were under constant attack from settlers, Tecumseh had witnessed first hand the lengths the whites would go to in order to acquire land. His tribe was among those relocated as the settlers moved into the Ohio Valley. The Shawnees had been pushed north-west when the British ceded the area to the United States. That was back when Tecumseh was in his early twenties. He knew what it was like for peoples to perish. Before the War of 1812, with the British backing him in their fight against the Americans, Tecumseh called on the Choctaws and Chickasaws, looking for warriors to join forces with him:

> But what need is there to speak of the past? It speaks for itself and asks, where today is the Pequot? Where the Narragansetts, the Mohawks, Pocanokets, and many other once powerful tribes of our race? They have vanished before the avarice and oppression of the white men, as snow before a summer sun.[32]

Angered by the series of land cessions by tribes, he called on those gathered to stand up, to unite and to hold on to what was theirs. Tired of raids and random massacres by the army and white settlers, yearning for a peaceful existence, and at times due to simple misunderstandings, tribes were continuing to sign treaties, ceding large plots of land. For Tecumseh, who knew first hand the unquenchable thirst of the white men for prime agricultural land and the lengths they would go to get it, what the tribes were giving up without a fight was unacceptable:

> Sleep not longer, O Choctaws and Chickasaws, in false security and delusive hopes. Our broad domains are fast escaping from our grasp. Every year our white intruders become more greedy, exacting, oppressive and overbearing. Every year contentions

spring up between them and our people and when blood is shed we have to make atonement whether right or wrong, at the cost of the lives of our greatest chiefs, and the yielding up of large tracts of our lands.[33]

It was a war cry, and, in a matter of months, that war would be fought. Zinn tells us that the War of 1812, referred to by traditional texts as a war against England for survival, was in fact much more than that: it was "a war for the expansion of the new nation, into Florida, into Canada, into Indian territory".[34] Jackson would become the war's hero, while Tecumseh would be killed in 1813 at the Battle of the Thames in Ontario and his confederacy would disintegrate.

The territory now gained, it needed to be cleared for the settlers. While war and pillage were ways of doing this, making use of the market economy was another option. Native tribes fighting alongside the Americans in return for the safety of their territories was a common phenomenon. In the Battle of Horseshoe Bend (1814) – in which Andrew Jackson annihilated the resisting arm of the Creeks known as the Red Sticks, whom he fought against with Cherokees on his side, later purchasing the Creek lands seized in battle – something new was brought into the equation. That same year, following the battle, Jackson would sign a treaty at Fort Jackson with the Creeks, which entitled individual tribe members to own land. This, Zinn tells us, was a move towards breaking up the communal nature of the native societies, aimed at "splitting Indian from Indian".[35]

The Treaty of Fort Jackson would sweep half of the Creek Nation's lands – prime cotton land – from under their feet. In the next decade, treaty after treaty would clear most of the southern part of the United States of native tribes, paving the road for a new set of professions that would keep Jackson's close circle of friends and relatives employed as "Indian agents, traders, treaty commissioners, surveyors, and land agents".[36]

Fever, disease, death

It was not only through invasion, warfare, self-serving treaties and intimidation that native communities suffered in their inter-actions with the whites: epidemics were also a major factor in depopulating areas, pushing some tribes to the point of extinc-tion and leaving others with dwindling populations, unable to defend themselves and thus forced to migrate. "The deaths of Indians," Wishart tells us, "especially of chiefs, priests, and doctors, eventually left holes in the cultural memory – visions were no longer explicated, ceremonies no longer practised, knowledge lost."[37]

Schlesier believes that, with early civilisations having already been wiped out in great numbers by diseases – possibly intro-duced to them through trade with their southern neighbours – and vast areas of previously inhabited land laying deserted, the explorers who arrived on the continent in the seventeenth cen-tury may not have encountered these empires in their original glory. These epidemics, travelling fast through human inter-action, had not only deprived the conquistadors and explorers of a fair assessment of the vastness of the former empires in the north, but also robbed them of the opportunity "to witness the associated density and complexity" of these societies.[38] That said, Schlesier claims both Cabeza de Vaca and Vásquez de Coronado were still lucky enough to observe "large, independent popula-tions". Others following the same route, however, would only find "scattered groups and much of the wide country devoid of people".[39]

A disease Schlesier rightly calls "the greatest slayer of Indian people", smallpox had already started infecting the inhabitants of the Americas as early as 1516, having arrived with the Spanish. It would soon become a pandemic, spreading throughout the continent. Cortez's men, immune to the disease, acted as porters, carrying the virus with them wherever they went. Once the virus took hold in a native community, it quickly spread to others through intertribal dealings.

"Because American populations had long been isolated from direct contact with the Old World, they were highly susceptible to virulent bacteria and viruses that had evolved there,"[40] Schlesier writes, adding that the death toll from smallpox alone was in the millions within a short period of time. Referencing anthropologist Henry Dobyns, he claims that this first round of the smallpox epidemic killed around "seventy five percent of the inhabitants wherever it reached".

In 1540, a Gentleman of Elvas would accompany Hernando de Soto into the Cofitachequi chiefdom. Written in the fashion of a travelogue and published in Portugal in 1557, his narrative is one of the better preserved early documentations of what explorers encountered as they travelled through Florida and South Carolina, eager to expand their trade in gold and slaves:

> The country was delightful and fertile, having good interval lands upon the streams; the forest was open, with abundance of walnut and mulberry trees. The sea was stated to be distant two days' travel. About the place, from half a league to a league off, were large vacant towns, grown up in grass, that appeared as if no

people had lived in them for a long time. The Indians said that, two years before, there had been a pest in the land, and the inhabitants had moved away to other towns.[41]

Mass mortalities due to sickness – "the pest" mentioned above – were considered ominous by tribesmen. Starting to believe the area they lived in was cursed, they would move, often not very far away, while keeping a record through the oral tradition of where the epidemic had struck their community. Not having the strength to move, certain tribes would undertake other drastic measures. Wishart mentions that the Omaha, afraid the disfigurement from smallpox would pass on to their children, "decided to launch a war party and die with some glory in a way that they understood". The tribe's warriors, all survivors of the 1800–1801 epidemic, waged war on "the Ponca, Cheyenne, Pawnee and Otoe," he writes, "until finally they returned to their Omaha Creek site to sow life again in the ashes of their past."[42]

As the fur trade gained prominence in the northern extremities of the Americas, the tribes in the Great Plains would become underpopulated due to a variety of infectious diseases. Their trading posts served as hubs where the natives were exposed to and contracted most viruses. This would lead to two smallpox epidemics in the 1800s as well as a cholera epidemic, which ran its course in 1849, wiping out a quarter of the Pawnee population.[43] The epidemic started in St Louis, killing roughly one-tenth of this bustling trading post's population. The official death toll for St Louis alone is today reported as 4,285, although this number probably doesn't count those who died of the disease but were buried outside the city limits.[44] The disease would soon be transported upriver, along with trade goods, on board the

Amelia, a steamboat belonging to the American Fur Company. Wishart tells us that "the traders knew cholera was on board, but they did not want to lose the season's trade. At each trading post cholera was unloaded with the cargo."[45]

Deaths through viral and bacterial infections were one way in which native peoples were perishing. An unfamiliar diet imposed on them in the reservations would soon become another. As the reservation system took hold in the late 1800s, to meet treaty promises the Federal Government would issue rations of flour, cattle and pork: food very much foreign to the tribesmen in the Plains. No longer able to hunt freely, forced to lead sedentary lives as farmers – an obstinate yet futile attempt by the government – families suffered intensely.

LaDonna, acting in her capacity as the tribal historian, talks about those early days:

> When the government made an agreement to say, "you guys gotta stay in this little square, you guys can't hunt, you guys can't do this, and we will provide the food", well, they sent us pork. And because pork is not indigenous to America, we did not have the enzymes to digest it, so it made us very ill. And then they gave us wheat. Flour, for bread, we did not eat bread. And then they gave us a lot of fatty fried substance foods, which we don't eat either, so it was a process of all of a sudden breaking our diets down, causing a lot of health issues.

Doug White Bull also tells us that diabetes is high on the list of diseases that kill native people in large numbers today: "when the white man first came, we didn't have diabetes. See, we ate, our diet was consistent of buffalo meat, low cholesterol, berries; we ate berries to flavour our food, we ate squash, healthy food we ate, you know." This food, he says, his people considered "medicine for our bodies". He mentions being shown by someone a photograph from the eighteenth century of a large group of Native Americans: "And he said, 'What do you notice about this picture?'. I said, 'They are all Native Americans.' 'Something else,' he said, 'look closely, there is not one obese Indian in that picture.' And so, after that, now, you don't find any skinny Indians, and it's all because of this food. This food is ruining our health."

The Seven Council Fires

The Lakota are the western arm of the Sioux[46] and consist of seven bands.[47] These seven bands join six other Council Fires to form the Seven Council Fires – Oceti Sakowin – and, thus, the original Sioux Tribe.[48] According to the Akta Lakota Museum and Cultural Center's webpage, the Oceti Sakowin, the name given to the largest camp during the Standing Rock resistance, and the significance of the sacred fire inside that was kept alive throughout the protests, can be described as follows:

> The original Sioux tribe was made up of Seven Council Fires. Each of these Council Fires was made up of individual bands, based on kinship, dialect and geographic proximity. Sharing a common fire is one thing that has always united the Sioux people. Keeping of the *peta waken* (sacred fire) was an important activity. On marches, coals from the previous council fire were carefully preserved and used to rekindle the council fire at the new campsite."[49]

Also on the official Facebook page of the Tribal Council for the Standing Rock Sioux Tribe today are the following statements:

The Standing Rock Sioux Tribe was defined by the Act of March 2, 1889 including all right-of-way, waterways, watercourses and streams running through any part of the reservation and to such others lands as may hereafter be added to the reservation under the law of the United States. The United States Government works in three levels: Federal, State and Tribal. The Tribal Government have a government-to-government relation with the United States. The Great Sioux Nation signed 1851 and 1868 treaties with the United States which are binding documents that retain our rights as a government.[50]

In the present day, the Lakota bands are scattered around the Great Plains in different reservations. The Standing Rock Sioux Tribe consists of a few bands of the Lakota and Yankton Sioux, who have been brought together by the Federal Government and settled within the continuously shrinking boundaries of their reservation. However, back in the day, and despite the signing of treaties and cessions of land, the Sioux Nation still (somewhat) freely roamed the Great Plains, and the tribal chiefs were determined to keep it that way at all costs.

It is said that on 25 June 1876, when Crazy Horse, the Oglala Chief and legendary warrior of the Lakota Sioux, called out to his man "Hoka hey! Today is a good day to die!",[51] more than a thousand warriors from the bands of Oceti Sakowin and the Northern Cheyenne rode across the Little Bighorn River, confident that it was the day they would claim victory once and for all against the white men. Sitting Bull, the Hunkpapa Chief and spiritual leader of his people, had had a vision. In his last Sun Dance, the wounds from which he was still recuperating on the day of the Battle of Little Bighorn, he had seen that his warriors would win. Black Elk would later recount those days preceding the battle:

> We camped there in the valley along the south side of the Greasy Grass before the sun was straight above; and this was, I think, two days before the battle. It was a very big village and you could hardly count the tepees. Farthest up the stream toward the south were the Hunkpapas, and the Ogalalas were next. Then came the Minneconjous, the San Arcs, the Blackfeet, the Shyelas; and last, the farthest toward the north, were the Santees and Yanktonais.[52]

The Lakota and Northern Cheyenne warriors who rode onto the battlefield confronted General George Custer and his group of 208 soldiers from the Seventh Cavalry, killing all but a few on first encounter. Custer died on the battlefield, and there were barely any survivors from the cavalry. Those who managed to escape hid in the bushes. Their access to water or a way out was cut off by tribesmen. Following an earlier rampage orchestrated by Custer, which saw the burning down and annihilation of Cheyenne and Sioux villages alike, this was a sudden and unexpected loss for the Federal Government. The *New York Herald*, on 7 July, would announce the General's death in capital letters: *MASSACRE – The Gallant Cavalry Leader's Death Officially Confirmed.*[53] On the same page was another headline: *The Autobiography of Sitting Bull.*

Much as the Red Cloud's War of 1866–68 was about preventing the establishment of the Bozeman Trail, which cut through Sioux lands to the goldfields of Montana, the Sioux Wars of 1876–77 were primarily about not giving up the Black Hills or the freedom to roam the Plains. From the Sioux perspective, the

Battle of Little Bighorn was just one in a series of conflicts, but one in which they had claimed absolute victory, and through which they believed they had made their point that the Black Hills was theirs. However, from the Federal Government's perspective, this loss called for severe punishment of the Sioux: both then and to this day.

In 1874, once Custer had found gold in the hills and assumed large deposits were buried under the rocky terrain, there was no way of stopping the gold rush that ensued. That and the Northern Pacific Railroad, which, Greene tells us, "penetrated into the Yellowstone River lands inhabited by the northern Sioux in the summer of 1873", were in fact harbingers of the Great Sioux War.[54] The settlers were keen on expanding into the Plains, all the way to the Black Hills, in order to exploit the land's hidden, underground resources. The native tribes had to be contained.

The Black Snake Prophecy attributed to the Lakota during the Standing Rock protests against DAPL is said to be an old story which predicts that a giant black snake will bring an end to the world. LaDonna talks about having heard of the prophecy when she was a small child:

> when we were children, we first heard the stories, we assumed what they were talking about. This black snake that will end the world was the internet systems that they were developing? And the black car they have been making on the road? I remember listening to Grandma and Ma talking, but how was the roads gonna end the world? Well, maybe they are gonna bring all bad people in. You know, I remember listening to the old people talking about this, what is the black snake? And so, and it wasn't 'til everybody

said, "It's oil, oil destroys the water, oil destroys the earth." They
said, "Oh, so that's what it is."

Back in 1876, the already completed Union Pacific Railroad
could possibly have been considered the "black snake" of the
time. To prevent the end of the world – their world – the tribes
united in what would be one last show of force, that is, until the
Standing Rock protests 140 years later. On the battlefield that
day, along the Greasy Grass,[55] an arrogant general couldn't foresee his fate, and neither could his administration in the east. The
battle was won thanks to a large gathering of tribes, a powerful
company not only boasting the support of legendary warrior
chiefs, but also, and more importantly, with faith on their side.
The *Wakan Tanka*[56] had granted Sitting Bull safe passage in a
vision, and through this his men and allies would ride to victory
on the day of battle. The Great Sioux Reservation, established
with the signing of the Fort Laramie Treaty in 1868 (marking the
end of Red Cloud's War), along with the Federal Government's
plans to confine the Sioux tribes into a set area, forcing them to
settle and become sedentary, would have to wait a bit longer.

The Federal Government's response to the result of the battle was cruel. The atrocities and massacres that the army conducted following the defeat of the Seventh Cavalry and the death
of Custer grew in intensity, with larger guns being introduced to
the battlefield. The powerful alliance of native peoples had dis-
banded after the victory at Greasy Grass, and this made it easy
for the US Army to corner and annihilate the Sioux bands, loot-
ing and burning villages, forcing masses to flee and killing those
who couldn't. Those the army captured were either arrested or
forced to return to the reservations. This manhunt, coupled with

insufficient bison and other wild game in the Plains to sustain the Lakota, not to mention the pressing hunger of bands existing outside the reservations, would finally culminate in the involuntary migration of the tribes to the reservation, and the surrender and brutal murders of Crazy Horse and Sitting Bull that followed.[57] The fear, fury and hatred that the Federal Government unleashed on the native population through its army would continue once the battle smoke had cleared away, through the acts of its agents, placed in reservations with the aim of subjugating the Indian.

Until the resistance at Standing Rock, the Battle of Little Bighorn was remembered as the last time the tribes tasted such absolute victory against the whites. So, in 2016 – more than a century later – when an even larger gathering of the tribes took place along the banks of the Missouri River, standing in solidarity to beat the "black snake" or at least delay its ominous visit; when a movement began to rise on the shoulders of native women and youth, the Federal Government once again failed to foresee what would happen. The land and all that lay underneath belonged to the many tribes who still roamed these lands, and the Lakota, the last of the region's original inhabitants, cared little for the oil. They believed in *mni wiconi*. They believed that water, not oil, was life. So, in spite of the corporate world of speculation and profits, the Lakota once again chose life.

"The Incident at Oglala"

We drive through the Badlands amid a snowstorm. The landscape we pass is impressive and almost deserted. The road is covered with a thick ice shield, and the falling snow continues to cover our surroundings in white, quietly adding to the area's magnificence, making it seem almost other-worldly. If not for the occasional car driving past us in the opposite direction, it would be easy to believe we are the last of human kind inhabiting this planet.

As we enter the Pine Ridge Indian Reservation, the road we are on takes us directly to a junction with red wooden signs on its banks, announcing our arrival at the Wounded Knee massacre site. Written on billboards, partially covered in snow, is a short version of the events of that ominous day, 29 December 1890. Beyond us lies the place where it all happened, an open space, eerily empty with only wooden posts acting as shade poles: a silent promise of warmer days. The tops of the posts jutting out from the prairie are covered with dried leaves and branches. An occasional bundle of sage hanging from one of the posts moves slowly in the wind. The metal hooks on horizontal wires between the posts, acting as bulletin displays, are a reminder that this place, the site of a massacre, is now a tourist attraction. With the falling snow, the place is as peaceful as death.

Except for the wooden posts, the site is plain, open ground. There are no hills or rocks in the immediate vicinity, or any other obstacle that could act as a cover or shield from an attack. So, back in 1890, when hundreds of civilians, women and children among them, were mercilessly slaughtered here by the US Army with Howitzer guns, they did not stand a chance. In 1975, when a seventy-one day siege in protest of the racist attacks on the Oglala – as well as the Federal Government once again breaking its treaty promises – culminated in the siege and shoot-out that ensued at the Jumping Bull compound, resulting in the deaths of two Federal Bureau of Investigation (FBI) agents and a young Native American named Joe Stunz, that trauma was revisited.[58]

The shared histories of the native peoples of the Great Plains are laced with stories of massacres and unruly attacks by the US Army on unarmed, peaceful civilians. As previously noted, the Battle of Little Bighorn stands out among these stories as a unique victory for the tribes. It is a story of not only courage but also cooperation, where coming together against a mutual enemy succeeds in overcoming all obstacles. Standing Rock is often referred to as this battle's twenty-first century successor, a peaceful reenactment of sorts. However, Standing Rock is not the only attempt by Native Americans in the Great Plains to reverse Federal Government decisions that directly affect their livelihood. There were several other instances prior to this.

One such reaction was the Ghost Dance movement,[59] the Federal Government's handling of which would eventually culminate in the massacre at Wounded Knee. Tribesmen, women and children would be slain by the Seventh Cavalry, the survivors of Custer's former regiment, looking to avenge the death of their commander. What began as a peaceful, prayerful gathering was suppressed by use of excessive force by the US Army, with civilians being literally mowed down by heavy artillery. The Wounded Knee Massacre would haunt the Lakota for years to come.

The intensity of the dances, the growing interest in them by the tribesmen, and the reports of dancers going into trances and having visions had all been too much for the eastern bureaucrats, who at the time were eager to complete white expansion into the Great Plains without any further problems. The ghost dancers were perceived as a threat, the dancers themselves looked upon as savages harbouring alternative, bellicose motives. Following the Battle of Little Bighorn, the Federal Government feared *any* gathering of tribes, let alone one as large as that now congregating at Pine Ridge. With the Ghost Dance movement, their fear would reach epic proportions, bordering on paranoia.

The Federal Government had enough of a reason to expect retaliation from the Lakota. Memories of their people being forced to sign away their land during the 1889 land commission were still fresh among the tribesmen. The last straw had been the killing of Sitting Bull in 1890 by Indian policemen acting on orders from the Indian agent at Standing Rock, James McLaughlin. McLaughlin had always considered Sitting Bull a threat; now, with the spread of the Ghost Dance movement, in his eyes that threat was even more imminent. Following up on intelligence that the Lakota chief was getting ready to visit the movement's leaders at Pine Ridge, and with a green light from the War Department, McLaughlin ordered Sitting Bull's immediate arrest.

The attempted arrest would lead to the murder of the Hunkpapa chief, with his unexpected assassination in turn creating a wave of panic in Washington. This panic was evident in the statement that Byron Cutcheon of the Committee on Military Affairs made at the House of Representatives. Cutcheon highlighted that it was indeed the "Secretaries of War and of the Interior" who had been requested to send the House "all official statements and correspondence in their possession, or that of their subordinates, relating to the arrest and killing of Sitting Bull, especially the reports of those officers and agents directly concerned in ordering or effecting the arrest of said Sitting Bull, together with all other papers or facts known to them in connection with said matter".[60] Aware of the controversial circumstances surrounding the assassination, Cutcheon, by backing the actions of the two ministries, seemed to be desperately trying to absolve his committee of any responsibility in the matter.

Unsurprisingly, the subsequent government correspondence and Agent McLaughlin's written account of the events leading to the killing of Sitting Bull became the official record of this event in governmental archives, once again whitewashing history. This version ran as follows: Indian policemen engaged in a firefight with the hostile Sioux, who refused to surrender their chief. Sitting Bull and seven of his men and six Indian policemen were killed on that day, with several others being wounded. Upon the death of the legendary Lakota chief, families fearing further repercussions from the US Army fled Standing Rock, joining the already growing crowd of ghost dancers at Pine Ridge Reservation.

Anthropologist Raymond DeMallie, an expert on the history of the people of the Great Plains, explains how the Lakota perceived the Ghost Dance movement. He states that the participation of the Lakota Sioux in the movement had largely started around Autumn 1890, and mainly due to similar concerns as those of the followers of Sitting Bull.[61] Despite official allegations that the ghost dancers represented a potential for armed resistance, DeMallie points out that:

> when the record is evaluated objectively, it seems clear that the Lakota ghost dance did not have warlike intentions. Hostility was provoked only when Indian agents demanded that the dance be stopped, and violence came only after extreme provocation – the assassination of Sitting Bull by the Standing Rock Indian Police and the calling in of the army.[62]

Stressing that the Ghost Dance movement cannot be dismissed simply as a reaction to the land cessions and prevailing hunger that the tribes were suffering at the hands of their oppressors, DeMallie asserts that it would also do it an injustice to describe it as a "desperate attempt to revitalize a dead or dying culture". Instead, he tells us that, although the movement is of foreign origin, it is crucial to include it in the "integral, ongoing whole of Lakota culture and its suppression as part of the historical process of religious persecution led by Indian agents and missionaries against the Lakotas living on the Great Sioux Reservation".[63] The subsequent annihilation of the native population at Wounded Knee by the military arm of the Federal Government, however, would serve as the ultimate punishment for the victory of the tribes at Greasy Grass, extinguishing the Lakota's last glimmer of hope for wriggling out of the *wasichu*'s grasp.

With the memory of the massacre still hanging thick as fog in the air, in 1973, 200 members of the American Indian Movement (AIM), upon invitation from the Oglala Sioux Civil Rights Organization (OSCRO), would show up and host a demonstration within the Pine Ridge Reservation, symbolically at Wounded Knee, demanding the impeachment of Dick Wilson, the President of the Oglala Sioux Tribal Council (OSTC). The full-blood and traditional Oglala communities were convinced that Wilson was not only corrupt but also favouring mixed-bloods over "traditionals" at Pine Ridge: a quality that made him a white agent from the Lakota perspective.

Historian Akim Reinhardt describes OSCRO as "a local, Indigenous, grassroots organization that opposed Wilson and Superintendent Stanley Lyman and resented the presence of armed federal law enforcement officers on their reservation".[64] It was formed thanks to full-blood Lakota elders such as Ellen Moves Camp and Gladys Bissonette. According to Reinhardt, these women were the "driving force" behind OSCRO: "while men have traditionally held the sanctioned offices of power in Lakota politics, women have often guided the development of various policies and spurred the men on to action, especially when they have perceived their men to be halting".

For years at the reservations, agents appointed by the Federal Government as its representatives favoured those whom they thought were easy to assimilate, while persecuting communities that held on strongly to their roots. So, having their very own, chosen tribal chairman undertake similar measures was nothing short of treason to the Oglala. This coupled with the fact that he was a nepotist, using tribal money for his own gain, warranted his impeachment. Wilson's 1990 obituary, which ran in the *New York Times*, would also revisit the stand-off at Wounded Knee: "The 300 occupiers charged that he was dictatorial and corrupt and that Mr. Wilson's administration was too cosy with the Government."[65]

As the Oglala got organised and started protests against Wilson, the Federal Government, in a typical fashion, filled the area with armed forces. During the unrest leading up to the impeachment hearings at Pine Ridge, the members of OSCRO stood alone against Wilson's armed militia, or GOONs – self-titled Guardians of the Oglala Nation – acting in unison with the FBI, the United States Marshals Service and the US military. It would be some time before AIM could fully take part in the events unfolding at the Oglala reservation, however. They already had their hands full.

AIM had formed in Minneapolis in the 1960s, primarily in response to the growing number of racist attacks on native communities and relentless police brutality. When Raymond Yellow Thunder, a fifty-one-year-old Oglala man, was publicly humiliated, mercilessly beaten and left to die by local thugs in Gordon, Nebraska in February 1972, AIM would come into limelight. Due to the movement's relentless protests, the arrests of the perpetrators would be guaranteed – albeit reluctantly – and what would customarily be slap-on-the-wrist charges would be upped to second-degree manslaughter. However, Raymond's death was neither the first nor the last hate crime to take place. So, when OSCRO finally called on AIM for help at Pine Ridge, they did not hesitate to answer. The battle lines were drawn. It would be the members of AIM and their sympathisers, along with the traditional Oglala of Pine Ridge, against a mix of Wilson's GOONs and federal armed forces. Thus, by the early 1970s, Pine Ridge was a battle zone. Random attacks, murders of natives, harassment of opposition members and shoot-outs at the reservation had escalated following the botched attempt to impeach Wilson. In 1974, he would be guaranteed another term in office. By that time, the violence at Pine Ridge would have left hundreds dead and arrest warrants issued for almost all members of AIM taking part in the resistance.

* * *

The second time we pull up to the intersection where the massacre site is located, trying to plot our return route to Rapid City on our smartphones, a battered old black car with a busted taillight pulls up near us, blocking our exit. The young woman in the driver's seat asks us whether or not we are lost. She is easy-talking, rolling words around a mouth that lacks several teeth, her remaining ones either broken or decayed. In the back seat of her car, several small children and a baby stare at us from a fogged-up window. We tell her we are not lost but looking for an alternate return route. She asks us, "Have you seen the Wounded Knee massacre site?". We say, yes, we have.

Standing out there in the snow, I think about what LaDonna told us a couple of days ago at Standing Rock:

So, we are 2.3 million acres, we are large land base, our community is so spread out, so it's really like, it's difficult for elders, it's difficult for people in general to get around. And if you don't own a car, and even if you do, can you afford the gas? It costs a lot of gas driving from one end of the reservation to another. A lot of people will save up their gas money just to make it to a doctor's appointment, and, or an appointment at the agency or the tribal office, cos it's a big thing to come from the communities.

Today, Pine Ridge Reservation is similar to Standing Rock Sioux Reservation, being one of the poorest places with the highest unemployment rate in the state of South Dakota. The public transportation systems servicing reservations are poor at best, so most families own cars. However, as LaDonna says, the price of gas does not come cheap for those who are already living below the poverty line.

As we continue to fiddle with our smartphones, which are useless when there is no cell reception, as is often the case in the heart of the reservations, the young woman in the battered old black car gets out and walks over to us. Holding a plastic box in her hands, she asks whether or not we would like to buy some of her arts and crafts. She then opens the box and pushes it towards us. Inside are small, delicate dreamcatchers with bright blue beads woven into them. She tells us that she sells them at twenty, thirty dollars apiece. She adds that she needs money for gas. I look at the small kids sitting in the back seat, staring at us expectantly. Right then, an older woman, who is sitting in the passenger seat, gets out of the car, carrying another dreamcatcher: plain, beautiful, with no beads on it, but displaying intricate handwork. My friend buys it, and we thank them. The younger woman then advises us to take the main road back. She says that, with the snow, the side roads will most likely be blocked. As we drive away, I look behind me via my rear-view mirror. I see them in the snow – two women, one old, the other looking older than her age – standing by their car, watching us leave. Standing at the junction in the snow like that, they look like the ghosts of another era.

BOX 5. A piece of old history in the "New World"

Massacres by the US Army are still vivid in the memories of Native Americans, the stories having survived via their oral tradition for at least seven generations. So, when DAPL came knocking, there was one more massacre the Standing Rock Sioux Tribe decided to put back on record for Corporate America: the massacre at Whitestone Hill by General Sully and his troops on 3 September 1863.

So, on 30 September 2014, as the tribal representatives sat in a meeting with officials from Dakota Access and Energy Transfer Partners, Tribal Historic Preservation Officer for the Standing Rock Sioux Tribe Waste'Win Young told them, "it's important that the land and the waters that we are talking about are not taken out of context. We have a really rich history here." She added, "our history and ceremonies are who we are. There's [sic] sixty-six village sites along the Missouri River within the boundaries of the Standing Rock Sioux Tribe." Young continued by describing the borders of the current-day reservation, stressing:

these lands were also home to the Arikara, Mandan, Hidatsa and the Cheyenne. The proposed Dakota Access Pipeline would cross the Missouri directly underneath a village site. There is an island that gets exposed when the Oahe Reservoir levels drop. This island is part of a larger village that is presently inundated. There are human remains, artefacts, pottery shards, tools throughout this entire channel. Across the Missouri River on the eastern shoreline, where [there were] Dakota camps including Chief Two Bears' and Little Soldier's camps, this crossing is near what was called Many Horse Head Bottoms. It's where the Dakota escaped Generals Sibley and Sully in 1863 after the massacre at Whitestone Hill.[66] Chief Big Head's family crossed the water here. When night fell, the babies were crying and the young girls carried them across the river; they plugged their nose[s] so they wouldn't be heard crying. They swam across the Missouri River with those babies. This is a story that many of us do not know, but it is an important part of our story that needs to be put out there.

Young paused briefly before continuing:

I actually struggled with this last night, is that do we want to tell something so important and sacred to us, to a pipeline company? But it's important for you guys to know the history and our connection to this area. Today, Chief Big Head's descendants are in the room. Chief Little Soldier's, as well as many of the descendants of a lot of other chiefs. And for us to officially endorse or accept a proposal that would negatively impact our cultural sites, our prayer sites, our duties and responsibilities as stewards of the land, it would be unacceptable and goes against the very intent of our office and in fighting and protecting and preserving what we have here, what we have left for our people and our children. And I thank you guys for coming, but the risks are too great for our children.

FOUR | Showdown at Standing Rock

The sacred hoop means the continents of the world and the people shall stand as one. (Black Elk)

A Dakota man married an Arikara woman, and by her had one child. By and by he took another wife. The first wife was jealous and pouted. When time came for the village to break camp she refused to move from her place on the tent floor. The tent was taken down but she sat on the ground with her babe on her back. The rest of the camp with her husband went on. At noon her husband halted the line. "Go back to your sister-in-law," he said to his two brothers. "Tell her to come on and we will await you here. But hasten, for I fear she may grow desperate and kill herself." The two rode off and arrived at their former camping place in the evening. The woman still sat on the ground. The elder spoke: "Sister-in-law, get up. We have come for you. The camp awaits you." She did not answer, and he put out his hand and touched her head. She had turned to stone! The two brothers lashed their ponies and came back to the camp. They told their story, but were not believed. "The woman has killed herself and my brothers will not tell me," said the husband. However, the whole village broke camps and came back to the place where they had left the woman. Sure enough, she sat there still, a block of stone. The Indians were greatly excited. They chose out a handsome pony, made a new travois and placed the stone in the carrying net. Pony and travois were both beautifully painted and decorated with streamers and colours. The stone was thought "wakan"(holy) and was given a place of honour in the center of the camp. Whenever the camp moved the stone and travois were taken along. Thus the stone woman was carried for years, and finally brought to Standing Rock Agency, and now rests upon a brick pedestal in front of the Agency office. From this stone Standing Rock Agency derives its name. (Legend of Standing Rock)[1]

One more round

"So. For me, there are levels. Everything has levels. So, we have this political level, and those political people need to be on that political level. So, we have the council, the governor and all these guys on this level. I'm not that level," says LaDonna, using her hand to draw the hierarchy of her society as horizontal lines in the air. Starting at the top, she continues: "This level, and they are negotiating, President of United States, you know, all these people. Then you have this level, which are all our spiritual people, the prayer people and stuff. Then you have this level, which are all the people working in the camp, the craft people, the builders, etc." By this time, having reached the bottom, she concludes: "Then you have the level I'm at. Feeding people. And that's how I look at it."

The acknowledged importance of women in Lakota culture manifests itself as bouts of female leadership during times of crisis. As in the movement at Standing Rock, along with OSCRO at Wounded Knee prior and several other indigenous movements arising from distress or as desperate attempts to protect the environment, women often play a central role, shouldering the struggle and assuming leadership roles that come naturally to them.

Wishart mentions this special power, which women continue to hold in native societies to this day. Although they assumed a subordinate role in the political structure of the tribe, he tells us that women, especially in the lodge, "had positions of authority and respect". Most importantly, they held ownership of "the lodge, the tipi, and most of its contents, a right of ownership that American women did not have until after the middle of the nineteenth century. The women also owned the fields, seeds, and implements of production." There was a hierarchy among the wives, and seniority was respected, especially in decision-making on internal matters such as "the distribution of food" or deciding where to set up their campsites and "tipis in relation to other members of the clan" during hunting season.[2] So, while men largely decided upon external matters such as warfare and hunting, it was mainly the women who ran the family unit. Thus, it was not a shock that LaDonna stood up when Corporate America came knocking with a threat of not only polluting the water but also disturbing the burial sites of her family, of her son Philip; nor was it a surprise that other native women, elders and youths alike, stood alongside her.

"Remember *mni wiconi*: water of life is female," she tells us, reminiscing about those days:

> and through this water, we bring children into this world. Through this water we care for all our children. We feed them, we clothe them, we wash them. Through water we bring life. That is why water is female. That is why it's our obligation to stand up. It's our obligation to protect that water. It is so easy for the men to destroy the water. It's the women who must protect the water. So it's in our culture that's ingrained in us. Water is life. Children are life. Women bring life.

LaDonna then goes on to explain how, in the camps and throughout the movement, they took special care to keep men who were known to be abusive or had been involved in a criminal act towards a woman or a child out: "Because this movement is exactly what, if you can abuse a woman, you can destroy the water. If you can abuse a woman, you can destroy the earth. If you can abuse a woman, you will not care what the Seven Generations have. But wait, that's how society is today. And so how do we flip that back around, so water becomes life, and women become life again?"

For most women who were at the front line of the struggle at Standing Rock, being part of it all – standing up for water, for life, for the Seventh Generation – did not only come naturally but was the only option. Once they took charge, they realised they wouldn't be standing alone. However, as LaDonna recalls, those days weren't easy: "Nothing is easy. There were problems with this movement. You know, people were, 'Oh, what are these women doing?' We have no choice. We have *no* choice."

In June 2016, she continues, "all the women who protect the water, we all met in New York City … they put out a call for all the women who carry and protect water and they invited me." There, LaDonna says, she met "all of these women from all over the world. And we were given a directive to bring our water from our rivers. And so we came, and just as we got there Hawaiians who canoed across the whole world came in with their water from Hawaii." There, united, the women prayed "to change the world. And it's not one person, it's everybody. So this is something way bigger than we have ever thought or imagined. But I didn't even know what happened here." LaDonna ponders: "the core we know. You stay in your area, grandma; grandmas rule, grandmas go forward, grandmas will do everything in the world to make sure the next generation is taken care of. So, all of that has to do with water."

While talking about her role at Standing Rock, LaDonna – although humbly downplaying the amount of courage it took for her to take action on that first day – doesn't shy away from pointing out the responsibility her cultural position laid on her: "I'm a grandma," she asserts once more. "In my culture, the grandma is the final voice for everything. So, who were the strongest people in that camp? All the grandmas. The grandmas were willing to die. They are willing to give up their lives for these guys. That's it, grandmas first. So, we are pure grassroots level."

And "willing to die" was not a sentimental exaggeration either. As groups of people from several different tribes, having shared a similar background of attempted assimilation, started to find their voices through the movement at Standing Rock, and as camps started springing up across the site where Dakota Access had positioned their machinery prior to construction, Washington became alert. Here, the Cherokee standing with the Sioux standing with the Dine, bolstered by their joint past, were staging a protest that was not only calling an end to centuries of exploitation, but also reminding the world what was most sacred and most necessary for our survival: water. What was going on at Standing Rock was bigger than what went on at Wounded Knee, bigger than any of the battles the Native Americans fought against white oppression. What was going on at Standing Rock was universal. The result of the battle to protect the water inside the Oahe Dam would, for better or worse, affect our planet, our livelihood. Thus, the movement broke free of its initial designation as a regional stand-off and found an international response.

At first, the Federal Government tried to block the protests through intimidation: measures taken against the water protectors consisted of a combination of armed private security and state police, situated north of the reservation, to "protect" the construction process from protests. Although solidarity inside the Sioux Reservation was too strong to give into fear, those across the river would nevertheless put it to the test. Intimidation tactics were soon employed, with unarmed protestors being gassed, charged at by attack dogs and, as the incorrigible Dakota winter took hold, blasted by water cannons at sub-zero temperatures in an attempt to contain and discourage them.

Recent disclosures by investigative reporting site *The Intercept* also shed light on the role played by a private contractor known as TigerSwan, who was hired by Energy Transfer Partners. The security firm's website reveals it was founded in 2007 by retired members of the United States Delta Force, and that it offers services which "identify and mitigate risks throughout the corporate operating environment".[3] According to a series of articles *The Intercept* ran in May 2017, based on information from internal documents leaked to them as well as intel obtained through public records requests, TigerSwan "targeted the movement opposed to the Dakota Access Pipeline with military-style counterterrorism measures, collaborating closely with police in at least five states".[4] The online news site claimed the company, at the time operating without a license, was collecting information on protesters, planting informants among them to both tap into information on the ground and create "divisions" where necessary. This series of articles provides visuals from situation reports – or "sitreps", an acronym used primarily by the military – that the security firm was issuing on a daily basis. *The Intercept* also reports on internal communication documents in which the security company suggested correlation between the water protectors and jihadists, framing the movement as having a strong ideological base that stems from radical religious motifs. Intimidation tactics, manipulation, harassment: at Standing Rock, none of these would work, at least not for long. The protectors would stand their ground as many more joined their fight, both physically and virtually. However, what the news site discloses in their series of reportage are the same concerns the water protectors also voiced at the time, mostly through social media, in order to warn each other.

As with many movements today, Standing Rock found its voice on the internet. As soon as the gathering in the Great Plains was underway, several Facebook pages were launched by individuals in support: advocating the cause, calling for donations or simply relaying information. Various web pages detailing the events at the reservation could also be found through a simple Google search. The word spread and stories were heard through the virtual grapevine, with live coverage of both daily life in the camps and the assaults on innocent bystanders. As with all things virtual, there also was lots of misinformation – false claims, exaggeration and accusations – both from participants and those who stood in opposition to the protests. Evidence was everywhere, but so were rumours masquerading as facts. One thing, however, was obvious: Standing Rock was no longer invisible.

Turning a protector into a warrior

As the movement grew, tension between the camp residents and the police force grew as well. And when heavy machinery belonging to the pipeline construction crew started digging up the area north of the reservation on 3 September 2016, things went from tense to violent overnight. The area being bulldozed was the sacred burial ground to which LaDonna referred in her original cry for help back in April, and of which Waste' Win Young had specifically pointed out the sacred nature – rich in historical artefacts and human remains – in her September 2014 meeting with the pipeline officials. This was also where LaDonna's son, Philip, was buried. Seeing her son's grave destroyed along with those of her ancestors was too much for the grief-stricken mother to bear.

Amy Goodman of internet news site *Democracy Now* soon went online with footage of the site being bulldozed and the subsequent confrontation between private security (with its attack dogs) and protesters.[5] The video shows men, women and children gathering along and soon going over a simple wire fence, trying to get close to the construction crew so they can yell at them to stop further disturbing the earth. Goodman then appears on camera, excitedly reporting from the site that "some of the security have dogs".[6] Her words are followed by vivid footage of a security dog running loose among protesters and trying to attack the horses of two civilian riders. Goodman continues to describe the scene to us: the bulldozers have moved away, having been replaced by security trucks. The people, despite being pepper sprayed, can still be seen standing their ground and chanting: "We are not leaving."[7] Soon, more join them. Goodman goes on to interview some of the protesters, who have fresh scars from dog bites on their forearms.

Democracy Now's seven-minute-and-forty-six-second footage would soon go viral and offer proof as to who the real aggressors were that day. An *Associated Press* story which ran later in the day

reported the number of injuries on the security personnel's side
– four security guards and two attack dogs – as well as the protesters' side – six people bitten by dogs, including a small child,
and at least thirty people pepper sprayed. The clash had taken
place less than a mile from where the water protectors camped
across from the construction crew. The article highlighted the
curious timing of the aggression: the Tribal Council had recently
filed in court their finding of "sites of 'significant cultural and historic value' along the path of the proposed pipeline".[8] The article
quoted Tribal Preservation Officer Tim Mentz pointing out that
"the tribe was only recently allowed to survey private land north
of the Standing Rock Sioux Reservation". He stressed that, during the surveys, "researchers found burials rock piles called cairns
and other sites of historic significance to Native Americans".[9]

The confrontation between the water protectors, the construction crew and their private security would be crowned by
the police making arrests over the course of several weeks. One
of those arrested was LaDonna's daughter, Prairie. The young
woman later recounted her arrest and her confinement in detail.
"At some point, a few of us were declared persons of interest,"
she said as she started going over the events of that day: "There
was a lock down or action we were trying to get to. As we left
Sacred Stone Camp, the yellow helicopter followed us. We got to
Highway 6, took a left on a county road. Three cops passed us,
immediately turned around on us."

Prairie said the police tailed them for about five miles before
speeding up to catch them: "When they pulled us over, they said
we were speeding. I said we never went over fifty. Then he said
we didn't slow down at the county bridge." Then, one of the
police officers reached in through the driver's window and tried

to grab Prairie's boyfriend, Anthony, "so Anthony jumped out and punched the cop's hand away. He said, 'Don't ever touch me unannounced.'" He then asked the police officer if he was under arrest, and when the police officer told him he wasn't, Prairie said that Anthony asked for his speeding ticket and their leave.

The young woman continued to recount the series of events, adding that while all of this was happening, "my mother was calling. I was able to answer my phone. And two cops opened my door unannounced and grabbed me, yanked me out backwards. So I started to fight back. Struggling, they handcuffed me. Put me in the back of the deputy police car." She remembered one of the police officers had a badge showing that he was from Fargo, North Dakota: "He said, 'Why did you resist? I'm so sorry, if this was in Fargo, this wouldn't be happening to you.' I said, 'I really don't know.'"

Arrested, Anthony and Prairie were taken to the police station, where they were forced to remove their shoes. Here, Prairie said she got worked up: "I've never been to jail except once on Standing Rock," she said, adding, "I'm not a criminal." The officers at the police station took Anthony to his own cell, Prairie continued, "and me to a room. Two women jailers told me to take my clothes off. I said no. I said, 'Maybe after you turn around, I'll kindly change.' The jailer said 'No, we are going to stand here and watch you get naked.' I said, 'My apologies, but I can't do that for you.' The jailer said, 'Take your clothes off or we will drag [you] out in the hallway and let the men watch too.'" Prairie answered this with a curse, "so they dragged me to the hallway where five men and two women started to try and strip my clothes from me". She added, laughing, "I resisted to the fullest."

Along the hallway into which she was dragged, she said there were "three solitary confinement cells", one of which contained

Anthony "watching the police strip me. After they got the cuffs on me, they started hurting me. Thumbs under your ear. Knees on my neck. I didn't breathe. Pressure points, whatnot." Prairie continued:

> they tried tearing my pants off but with the cuffs on, I managed to hold to my pants 'til they started hitting my hands. I screamed and cursed the whole time and my boyfriend listened to all of it. After they got my clothes off they walked out of the room and left me on a cement floor. I tried to lay face down but I was freezing. Then they came back and threw orange clothes at me. I'm guessing four hours later they came to book me. I watched them plug my cellphone into their computer and all my info show up on their computer. Just then the whole police station went into system failure!

She laughed again, before adding "someone said Anonymous hacked them".

The two of them would spend that night incarcerated. Prairie had her first hot shower "in a long time and I slept like a baby". Suddenly thoughtful, she added, "No wonder everyone likes jail. A bed and three meals and hot water." The next day, handcuffed and shackled, those arrested would stand in the hallway and wait for their indictment. "We asked what our bail was when we got there. Mine was $250 then. As we stood in the hallway, jailer said my bail was now $500." Prairie continued, "pretty soon, officer said our last names. 'McLaughlin, Story back in your cell.' Anthony asked why. Officer said, 'You two have no court.'" She explained that Anthony then asked a second time why they were not going to be taken to court, only to be told that their paperwork was not yet finished. She said her boyfriend, "got angry and said 'You have twenty-four hours to legally charge us. So if your paperwork isn't finished we aren't legally charged.'" He then demanded their release:

> We went to our cells for another twenty minutes. The officers came back. Said 'Story McLaughlin court.' As we got escorted in the court room, I heard the judge say 'Oh, these two, I heard about these two.' Then, I stood before her. She raised my bond to $750. At the time, it was the highest bond set so far since opening of camps.

As soon as Anthony went before the judge, Prairie added, he realised their charges had been changed: "what they arrested us for wasn't what we went before the judge for. I got a resisting charge and Anthony got obstructing a government's function. He got the cool charge."

The arrests of protesters from that September day onwards would continue well into October. In October 2016, the internet would ignite once more, this time with footage of the actress Shailene Woodley, recorded by the actress herself, being taken into custody for criminal trespassing. The broadcast spread across the internet like wildfire. As the footage showed, in the background, Morton Country Sheriff Office personnel were visible, heavily armed and standing by their armoured vehicles.[10] The police officer who was attempting to place Woodley under arrest in the video seemed rather unclear as to what she was being charged with, and someone off-frame was heard informing him that she was being charged with trespassing. Woodley objected, saying that she was on the property with hundreds of other people, so why was it that only she was being arrested?

The answer she received was a flat: "Because you have been identified."

Only a couple of weeks later, the front pages of several independent news sources once again lit up with the images of a peaceful march of solidarity met with disproportional police violence. The events of this day had in fact started with a large group of civilians gathering and trying to peacefully walk over to where construction equipment was lying in wait. This time, instead of private security, the marchers were met by police. The stand-off would end with the protesters being pepper sprayed, beaten, and – for several of them – arrested. *The Guardian* would later announce that the number of arrests on that day amounted to upwards of 120, and included many journalists and film makers.[11] A reporter writing for *The Intercept* vividly described the scene as follows:

> As the protesters attempted to leave, the police began beating and detaining them. Several Native American women leading the march were targeted, dragged out of the crowd, and arrested. One man was body-slammed to the ground, while another woman broke her ankle running from the police. The military and police trucks followed the protesters as nearly a hundred officers corralled the protesters into a circle. Among the arrested were journalists, a 17-year-old pregnant girl, and a 78-year-old woman.[12]

A year later, the *Bismarck Tribune* reported that 761 arrests were made throughout the protests at Standing Rock.[13] This article mentioned that of the forty-seven cases closed at the district court, thirty-three were dropped: the judge ruled that those charged with trespassing on private property on that day in

September 2016 were not given proper notice by the police that the land they were on was in fact private. Of these 761 arrests, a large portion were made later during camp closures. Following the September stand-off at St. Anthony, harassment by the police and the detentions that ensued at the height of the Standing Rock protests became almost customary. Travel anywhere close to the camps was hampered by police check points and roadblocks. Reporters were barred from covering the events,[14] and those at Standing Rock faced charges such as "criminal trespass" or "engaging in a riot" for simply doing their jobs.[15] The Committee to Protect Journalists would report that "the burden of legal costs or risk of further charges if they [were to be] arrested again" had discouraged many reporters from further covering the protests.[16]

On the legal front

It soon became apparent that waging a battle for clean water, and ultimately for survival, solely on the ground would not be sufficient. Realising this, the Standing Rock Sioux Tribe, with the Cheyenne River Sioux Tribe soon joining them, took the matter to court. The first move the Standing Rock Sioux Tribe made was filing an official complaint against USACE at the district court in July 2016, citing that the Army Corps had violated the Clean Water Act, the Rivers and Harbors Act and the National Historic Preservation Act (NHPA) by issuing a Nationwide Permit in 2012 (NWP12) that authorised "discharges into federal waters without ensuring compliance with the NHPA".[17]

The complaint read as follows: "DAPL crosses hundreds if not thousands of federally regulated rivers, streams, and wetlands along its route. The discharge of any fill material in such waters is prohibited absent authorization from the Corps." However, by issuing the Nationwide Permit, the USACE had "pre-authorized construction of DAPL in all but a handful [of] places requiring federal authorization without any oversight from the Corps. In so doing, the Corps abdicated its statutory responsibility to ensure that such undertakings do not harm historically and culturally significant sites."[18] Having received no satisfactory response to their complaint, in August 2016 the Standing Rock Sioux Tribe took USACE to court, demanding that it withdraw the NWP12.[19]

LaDonna had voiced her concerns on numerous occasions that the construction of DAPL would not only pose a threat to the water but also seriously disturb their sacred sites, causing unrecoverable damage. So, on the day we sat together in the Prairie Knights Casino and this subject came up, she became emotional. "There are 370 archaeological sites they have destroyed in the state of North Dakota alone," she pointed out. "I didn't count South Dakota, Iowa, Illinois. They have exterminated a thousand sites, that's burial sites, sacred sites, ceremonial sites, petroglyphs." Later, with desperation apparent in her voice, she asked, "and we are saying, are you guys terrorists?"

A corporation, with the strength of the US Army and Federal Government behind it, coming along and deciding it had the right to disrupt areas sacred to the tribes was a reminder of times past, and a sign that not much had changed in Washington with regard to its dealings with the native population. "Why do you have the right to take my footprint off my land?" LaDonna asked. "I have been here for thousands of years." After a brief pause, she added, "So, yes, we were upset. So they did not consult with us, there is no other pipelines in this area, and there will not be. And Dakota Access still does not have oil in that pipeline yet. It's yellow journalism."

Despite the legal steps taken by the Standing Rock Sioux Tribe against USACE and an easement to construct underneath the Oahe Reservoir pending, the construction company continued its work to complete the pipeline. However, in December 2016, mainly due to the public outcry, the growing number of protest camps at and around Standing Rock and President Obama's delayed recommendation, USACE would cave and not grant the easement that Dakota Access needed to cross the river. Unfortunately, this – as expected – offered only temporary relief, not an absolute victory. It only granted the tribes of Standing Rock and Cheyenne River some more time to shape their legal strategy.

In February 2017, all eyes and ears in the Dakotas were fixed on the White House when, through executive orders signed in front of cameras, President Trump – also as expected – gave the green light that DAPL needed. A few weeks after our talk with LaDonna, in May 2017, the headlines for local and national papers would announce that oil was now flowing through DAPL.

The easement granted by USACE to DAPL under orders from President Trump had also stopped efforts for a detailed Environmental Impact Assessment (EIA) dead in its tracks. Planned to be carried out prior to an easement being granted, and reinitiated under the old presidency, the EIA was no longer deemed necessary. The land that lay on the outer parameters of the present day reservation was once again up for grabs for white Corporate America.

On 14 February, acting on behalf of the Standing Rock Sioux Tribe, Earthjustice, a nonprofit environmental law organisation, filed a motion for a summary judgement on the lawsuit the tribe had filed against USACE, asking the judge to rule primarily on two issues that needed to be reconciled: "whether National

Environmental Policy Act requirements have been met and whether the Corps' actions violate the tribe's treaty rights". On the legal initiative's website, details of the case further explain the situation: "The judge appears ready to move forward on this case on an expedited basis, which is vital since attorneys for the Dakota Access Pipeline now say construction could be completed much sooner than they originally told the court."[20]

However, despite the legal steps taken by the tribes, by 22 February the camps scattered around the countryside would start to be emptied and closed down by force.

Eviction notice served
"So, on 4 December, we know that the chairman met with the Army Corps, Morton Country and the Governor. And all of a sudden, it was like a roundabout face, he changed everything," LaDonna tells us as she reminisces about the events that brought an end to camps such as Sacred Stone and the protests at Standing Rock as we knew them. "And we are not quite sure what happened, I don't have no idea, nor am I gonna say." She continues, telling us the chairman called a meeting at which "he said, 'I think everybody should go home.' I said, 'My camp is different, we are starting a green energy camp. We are not a protest camp.' But he kept lumping us in."

This controversial call by the chairman would, at the time, bring heavy criticism down upon him; it would be perceived that he, of all people, was giving up the struggle, or, worse, was changing sides. The Tribal Council soon announced through social media that the water protectors should leave for their own good, stressing that most of those in the makeshift camps were not prepared for the Dakota winter. However, despite the harsh weather and dropping temperatures, the self-proclaimed water protectors on the ground were determined to stay. The oncoming winter would only add to the challenges they already faced.

LaDonna remembers how everyone, against all odds, was trying to keep their spirits up. She humorously recalls one of her exchanges with a camp resident: "We have this man show up, 'Ah, you are not dressed for winter.' 'Oh, no, I've got…' 'No, you are not dressed for winter! We layer here, you put layers of clothes on. Do you understand where we live? If you are out, if your skin is exposed, you die!' You know, but we know how to live here." Laughing briefly, she continues, "So, for us, as the winter, as it gets colder, you know, when it gets about zero, then we actually pull out our winter coats. You know, cos we are used to the cold." But the camps lured all sorts of people, from all over the country and across the world, "that were not used to the cold, and no matter how much we tried to tell them, you gotta prepare, you gotta prepare…" In her camp, Sacred Stone, LaDonna adds, "I made sure everybody was prepared." She is a grandma after all.

Thus, when the chairman came to call with a state-issued eviction notice for the camps, LaDonna repeats that, at first, she objected, insisting that their camp was different. She stresses that when they were starting up the camp, they had relied on their own resources and not asked for any contribution from the tribe: "We did everything ourselves, which is really good, because we were self-sufficient compared to the other camp. And then as we raised money, we bought our belongings, while the other camp lived on donations. It's a different process."

She continues by telling us that they built alternative energy hubs such as wind towers and solar panels to provide the camp with ample energy, including a thermal energy setup for the school inside Sacred Stone: "It was so cool, cos they had this little chimney, and you would put wood in it there and it start burning, and it would heat the whole walls and floors." LaDonna gets excited when she talks about Sacred Stone. The camp turned into an idyllic project, a hope for the future and for the young people, who were building it up, brick by brick; the possibility of it all animates her as she continues: "We built root cellars, we prepared food for winter, people in my camp made food. We had two kitchens, one for us and one for vegetarians." Those at the camp were almost ready for a long-term stay. She tells us they had even "made deals with the organic farms, and they brought in produce, so we were in the process." She adds, "our next adventure was to be planting so that we could grow our own produce. We were working with getting solar panels. And so we were hoping to open in June of 2017, to start bringing kids and to teach them how to live off the earth. That is still our plan."

Sadly, that plan will be on hold for a little longer. Today, in the empty expanse of what used to be the campsite, except for the occasional bundle of sage hanging from bushes at the northern extreme, not a trace of what LaDonna describes remains. As we pull over to the side of the road, deciding to take a lunch break by the lake – alongside which only a few months ago stood many colourful tents, yurts and tipis – a helicopter appears almost out of nowhere. It flies low over us for a few moments before taking off, having decided we are not a threat. There are signs posted on the fence encircling the campsite that inform trespassers to stay out.

We enter the area that used to be the Sacred Stone Camp from an obviously man-made opening in a newly erected wire fence, indicating the presence of others who have visited the site before us. Later at the casino, LaDonna tells us that this was, in fact, her handiwork; she had taken some food with her down to the former campsite the previous week, to mark the anniversary of the camp being founded. Although she had not invited anyone along, people started showing up of their own accord, and soon there was a small gathering.

It's a sunny day when we stand at Sacred Stone, taking in the vast and desolate landscape that lies in front of us. LaDonna's description of the events leading up to the end of the protests still ring in our ears: "So, in January, there were all the rumours that they were gonna close the camps. The governor was doing some really awful things to people." Those awful things included arresting protestors, mostly on unfounded charges; mistreating them while in custody; harassing them; and blatantly violating their constitutional rights. "We continued on, cos, we figured, we are on the reservation. The other camp was not. It was off the reservation, so we didn't have jurisdiction." The other camp that LaDonna is referring to is Oceti Sakowin, founded along the banks of the Cannonball River, and one of the largest gatherings of people in and around the Standing Rock Reservation.

LaDonna's account of the governor's actions are not unfounded either. By the end of October 2016, there were many widespread claims by those arrested that humiliating strip searches targeting mainly non-whites were taking place,[21] along with allegations that those being taken into custody were being kept in cages.[22] These personal accounts of arrests, ongoing police violence on the ground and intimidation received a mention in a UN mission report from the Office of the High Commissioner for Human Rights. On 3 March 2017 – a few weeks after the camp closures – UN Special Rapporteur on the Rights of Indigenous Peoples

Victoria Tauli-Corpuz issued her end-of-mission report on her visit to the United States. In her report, she underlined "the criminalization of indigenous peoples asserting their right to protest in the now-world famous struggle of several tribes in opposition to the Dakota Access Pipeline."[23] She asserted that, "while the actions taking place have been almost completely non-violent and peaceful, there has been a militarized, at times violent, escalation of force by local law enforcement and private security forces."[24]

This militarisation of local law enforcement was omnipresent throughout the camp closures. LaDonna continues to tell us of the day they first heard talk of eviction at Sacred Stone: "15 February, they came here – at this table, in fact – and served me with the paper, saying that there were possible trespassers on tribal trust land. It was not an eviction notice, it was 'possible trespassers on tribal trust land'. And so we took it and they served people down here."

A decision had to be made among those at the camp. "I said, 'Well, what do we do?' And they said, 'Well, we are a prayer camp, we are in prayer, we will move.' So, we started on that day, tearing down. But you gotta understand, we had been there for a year. And so there is a lot of stuff."

Just as they started dismantling the camp and moving their belongings out, LaDonna says the police intervened, setting up a blockade: "they forbid us food and water, and we had about a hundred people who left, and we finally negotiated an allowance of five gallons of water". Soon after, however, "they told us that they were gonna totally stop allowing people in there, put up what they call a 'hard blockade' at noon." With the forced shutdown of the camps imminent, LaDonna says she went with a small group of people to help retrieve whatever they could salvage from Sacred Stone:

I had a whole tent of gourmet coffees and I was thinking 'Let's try to get as much coffee as we can out of there.' But we got up there, they came two hours early, and forbid us to go in. And then the chairman and them sent in his friends, and they took whatever was remaining, but what really hurt us was we had supply tents for brand new supplies. Sleeping bags, tents, solar panels, etc., and they took a bulldozer and bulled them all down. You see this pile of garbage? It's all brand new stuff. I was like, they could have given it to the community. And we had these big store areas built for food. They could've given the food away. But anyway, they didn't, so.

Waving her hand in the air in dismissal, she continues:

the police told us they would not tear down our kitchen, cos we just had built a brand new kitchen. And they would not tear down the school. And then they bulldozed the school and I think everybody was absolutely devastated, cos that was such a beautiful school, we had such a good time, the kids had such a good time in there. And so everybody is in different stages of grief. We were trying to follow the law, we were not the group that was protesting not to move; I know there are people over at the big camp that refused to move, but our people said we would move.

LaDonna's surprise over the destruction of her camp despite their compliance with the authorities is quite a familiar reaction. Hyde also mentions the dichotomy of compliance versus resistance time and time again when writing about the land cessions. His most poignant example is that of the Lower Brulé from the 1890 land commission. At the beginning of the events that led to a joint cession of nearly half the landmass encompassing the Great Sioux Reservation, the Lower Brulé had also thought that through compliance with and acceptance of the Commission's demands they would be able to protect their land. The band's leader, Chief Iron Nation, had even negotiated in person with General Crook. According to Hyde, the chief had gone so far as to obtain a written guarantee that, once the Land Commission was through with its dealings, the Lower Brulé would not be left homeless. However, they soon found this would not be the case, and in the end they were left worse off, losing all of their land and any claim to a reservation. The Lower Brulé lands would be divided up among white settlers, and, up at Rosebud, their Brulé brothers would refuse to give up any of their remaining lands for them to settle in.[25]

Many such examples of broken promises are scattered through the pages of the historical archives, and when we fast forward to today, we find that not much has changed.

Meanwhile, down at the Cheyenne River

It was late afternoon when we drove into an empty powwow site at the Cheyenne River Reservation, directly south of CRYP. On a grassy patch at the north-east end of the small, wooden circular structure – almost like a miniature stadium – were tents in different shapes and sizes. As we got out of our car and started walking towards them, a young man jumped off a ledge and approached us. He introduced himself, saying his name was Chris and that he was from Arizona. After a round of introductions, and a slightly timid welcome from Chris, he asked us what we were there for.

Our stop over at the powwow site had been a spur-of-the-moment decision. Our original plan was to head up towards Standing

Rock after our meetings at Cheyenne River; however, one of the staff at CRYP told us that a sweat lodge ceremony was happening at Eagle Butte, so, curious and eager to attend, we decided to stay the night there. Julie, who had prearranged plans to go to Rapid City, had already left as we checked in to one of the two motels in the small town. The ceremony was cancelled at the last minute, so – with some unexpected free time in our hands – we drove back to CRYP to hang out for a little longer. That's when we found out there were some water protectors parked within walking distance of the youth centre. This information piqued our interest. Despite having driven up and down Main Street numerous times since our arrival at Eagle Butte, their small campsite, surprisingly, had not stood out to us. So, when we arrived at the powwow site and a young man asked why we were there, we did not have a definitive answer – other than that we wanted to meet, in person, some of the people who had taken part in the struggle.

As we stood there trying to explain ourselves to Chris, a tall young man with a goatee, black clothes and combat boots who had been sitting with a few others some yards back got up and walked towards us. He told us his name was Will and that he was in charge of security at the small campsite. By now, Chris had already started telling us his story of hitchhiking all the way from Arizona to stand in solidarity with the water protectors. When asked what prompted him to come, he answered that he was "tired of the system". So, instead of working at a restaurant back home, he decided to come here and resist. The details of his departure resembled a mystic tale of some valiant knight going on a mythical quest. He told us that as he packed up and parted from his family, things got rather emotional. He responded to his mother's tears with a hug, and then, hugging both, told his parents that his decision to come here was final, that this was his "calling". Chris's family cried behind him, asking him not to go: "I told them I loved them very much but this was something I had to do."

Chris's quest was a personal one, much like those of most people – native and non-native alike – who had participated in the resistance. Having started his journey in March, the camps at Standing Rock long since closed, he arrived at Cheyenne River and joined the water protectors, who had mainly been pushed south following their eviction. Aware that the most heated days of protesting were over, and that most of the protectors had gone home, Chris's coming here seems to have been a rather desperate attempt to break from routine: an alternative to working for meagre wages at mind-numbing jobs, trying to scrape a living while keeping his head above the hunger line; still staying poor, with no hope for the future.

As Chris continued his story, Will, who had been standing alongside us all this time, fiddled with his phone. I remembered having seen him earlier, sitting on the ground in the parking lot of the motel where we had checked in, then also with his phone in hand, continuously messaging. Having already taken our names, he asked us the reason we were here. As we told him what we had already told Chris, he continued to multitask: talking into a walkie-talkie he had with him, announcing our arrival in choppy messages to whoever was at the other end, while continuing to punch further information about us into his phone. While we waited for him to finish his messaging in order to give us clearance, we stood there chatting to Chris for a bit longer. Despite trying to look all serious and businesslike, Will would eagerly join in the conversation whenever the topic switched to Standing Rock.

Soon, a man and a woman came into the powwow site carrying shopping bags. They welcomed and invited us with warm,
friendly smiles to what seemed like the camp's main structure,
a green military-type field tent, larger than the rest in the small
campground. Will, by now convinced that we meant no harm,
urged us on. As we approached, more people came out of their
tents to shake our hands and introduce themselves. They lin-
gered a bit, making small talk, and then left.

Foxy and Alton, as we found out the two newcomers were
called, tried to make us comfortable once we were inside the
tent, offering us seats, something to drink and even something
to eat. The interior was more spacious than it had appeared
from the outside. It was set up almost like a living room, with all
sorts of creature comforts readily available: cots, a comfortable
looking divan, a small television set with a satellite receiver, a
coffee machine, folding chairs, food stock and a large table over
which lay the scattered remnants of what looked like the previous night's dinner. The young couple positioned themselves
on the divan, Will dropped onto a cot next to them, and we
each took a chair. Alton then grabbed a large wooden shell and
started burning some sage in it. Once the dried herb caught fire
and started to smoke, he passed it around to the rest of us. Sitting in a naturally formed circle, we all took the fuming shell,
one person at a time, and let the purifying smoke wash over our
faces before passing it on.

As we sat there exchanging pleasantries, Chris entered the tent
carrying a five-gallon water bottle. He placed the drinking water
at the centre of our small congregation and uttered the words
"mni wiconi" in salutation. Those in the tent all responded in the
same manner, repeating the Lakota saying: water is life.

As soon as Chris left the tent, the topic switched back to Standing Rock, with Foxy telling us about her last days at the camps. Their memories of the evacuations still fresh, her and Will became emotional at times, but continued nevertheless. Talking about the destruction of their camp as if it had been an idyllic, sacred place that was lost forever – as if they had managed to steal a glimpse of heaven on earth, never to be seen again – Foxy and Will's story of the saddest days of the Standing Rock protests came spilling out.

The end…?

In February 2017, the Army Corps initiated a flood warning, using the unusually temperate Dakota winter as an excuse. Despite the moderate temperatures, the tributaries were still frozen and flooding wasn't imminent. However, the warning soon turned into an eviction notice issued by the State. On Wednesday 22 February, at around 4 p.m., riot police in full gear would close in on Oceti Sakowin. The orderly camp, once host to a population of hundreds of people, was by then partially empty, a ramshackle version of its once glorious self. Tents and stockpiles were set ablaze, burning as the protesters who still inhabited the camp waited grimly for police to move in. As LaDonna mentioned earlier, those who were standing their ground were determined to stay put.

Still not sure what to think of it, I asked why those at Oceti had chosen to burn their tents. At the time it was relayed that the protesters did not want to see their sacred structures being desecrated. Chris responded to my question by saying "to get rid of all that negative energy". For someone who had not been in the camps, those were some definitive words. Will, who had lived through the camp closures just like Foxy, was deeply affected by my question coupled with Chris' response: "I am afraid to go back," he said. He then broke down but continued to explain between sobs that having lived at Oceti, which was more of a home to him than anywhere else, and having belonged to that group of people meant his heart couldn't bear to see the camp in pieces.

Having been homeless for quite some time before he joined the movement, Will felt Standing Rock was central in regaining his dignity. In the camps, he was someone again; as he told us himself, he was "the guy in charge of security detail", a responsibility that added meaning to his life, a newly found sense of purpose that would make him believe in himself again. "Standing Rock changed me," he confessed. Talking about all that he had learned and encountered there, he couldn't keep from wondering: "How do you explain to someone what real repression looks like?"

Foxy also remembered eviction day at Oceti Sakowin clearly, and as we sat around inside that tent in the relative safety of Cheyenne River Reservation, she recounted those days of arrests, forced removals and chaos. She told us that Oceti was the largest camp by far, and first on the clearance route of the armed forces moving south. Eventually all of the protest camps that stood along the Cannonball and Missouri rivers lining the northern extreme of the reservation would be cleared. However, as Oceti was immediately outside reservation land, emptying it of water protectors would be the least complicated.

The young woman's memories of that day were fresh, as if what went down a few months ago had happened only yesterday. "I was trying to save the Seventh Generation kids," she said. The parents of the young protectors taking part in the movement had pleaded with her to save the kids first, to get them out before the police moved in on the camp area and started making arrests.

Foxy said the families had specifically told her to "save our kids, our children are no good to us in jail". So that was what she did. She told us that she led the children, along with the rest of the protesters who chose to comply with the eviction notice, across the frozen river to Rosebud Camp. Rosebud, located south of the Cannonball River and on reservation soil, was as yet undisturbed.

"The next day, we stood at Rosebud and waited for them [the riot police] to come in with their guns," she recalled, adding, "it was eerie at Rosebud." The next day, feeling unsafe, and with police now closing in across the river, Foxy moved to the Vortex, the next camp over from Rosebud along the Cannonball River. There they stayed for three or four days, before once again being forced to leave. They moved on to Sacred Stone. Here, they would stay for another three days, until that morning when the bulldozers and other heavy machinery showed up to mow the camp down.

Meanwhile, LaDonna was fighting with the tribal officials to save Sacred Stone. With that fight lost as well, and the razing of Sacred Stone imminent, Foxy told us that, taking the children with her, she moved on to the Seventh Generation Camp, and deeper into reservation land. By that time, all of the camps, both on and off reservation soil, were being evicted. As a final measure, she said, she sought refuge in the casino. Once inside, while all of the camps were being levelled, Foxy, feeling powerless to stop any of it, just slept through the rest of the mayhem.

When Sacred Stone was being torn down, LaDonna told us, they did not have much of a chance to intervene: "We took everybody to a protected area, and took what supplies we could keep. And the chairman has confiscated the rest of our supplies. With that, we are continuing on, because we are building a green village." At this point, she paused before contemplating:

How do you make a negative a positive? You teach people how to live off the earth again. Well, if you understand, we live in a world that fossil fuel is now our priority, we drive our cars, heat our homes, they make food out of it, they make all these things – plastic, whatever you want – so now what we can do in this time and space is start planning to learn how to live on earth to divest [*sic*] from it. We are not saying, today, tomorrow, don't drive your car, we are saying, make a plan, how do we want to see our future, and so that's where we are at.

Foxy, Will, Alton and the rest of those who were evicted from Standing Rock and took refuge at the small campground by Cheyenne River, it seemed, had temporarily hit pause on their lives. While staying in that small campground, they looked as if they were merely trying to decide what to do next. The months at Oceti had obviously changed them for life, and with all of that now lost to them, they seemed confused. While I sat there thinking all of this, as if having read my thoughts, Foxy raised her head and told me that, as they left Oceti Sakowin, they all took a piece of amber with them from the Sacred Fire. Her words made me realise I couldn't have been more wrong. That amber was what continued to light their path today.

...Or just a beginning?
"You know, for that period of time where we thought that we were taught that we shouldn't be Indian, we shouldn't look Indian, we shouldn't speak Indian, we shouldn't do those sorts of things," Julie tells us as we sit at CRYP, "it takes generations to fix that." We are talking about what she calls her "colonised brain", a notion that continues to split the community, and especially

the native youth of today. "You know, conflict resolution," she exemplifies what she is trying to explain to us: "I started looking at workshops, and all that sort of stuff, and then my cousin – who is a relative of mine at Pine Ridge – he said, 'I think what you are looking for is, like, Lakota way, the resolution', and I am like, 'You're right!' You know? But I forgot that." Julie believes that what both she and the native youth need today is to retrain their ways of thinking. "It didn't come to mind right away, and that's a product of every bit of history that has happened," Julie confesses. "Wouldn't that be great, if our little kids were a piece of that from the very early ages and it is a natural part of them? You know, just like getting up and getting dressed: being Lakota. That's a natural part of who they are too."

"I feel like, when it comes to oppressed people, there's maybe a process that comes after that," Tammy tells us, "there is a place where you are submissive and you are acceptive [*sic*] and you work with it, and there is a place where you get angry, and anger doesn't really solve anything. I think for a long time people were angry. And I think we've come to a place where people are beginning to let go of that anger and be able to work on it at a different level."

With that in mind, and working with kids one-on-one, Tammy, much like Julie, has been lucky enough to directly observe what the Standing Rock movement did for the youth and how it affected them. "At the beginning of that movement, it came from kids, you know, one of the kids who grew up in our system," she tells us, "Jasilyn, Jasilea and Joseph, all three of them." Jasilyn Charger and Joseph White Eyes were among those who stood at that meeting a year ago and told LaDonna they would help her set up the first camp. Tammy has known them, particularly the twin sisters Jasilyn and Jasilea, since their childhood. She tells us that she has watched them transition from teenagers to young adults. "What they have gone through, they've gone through some tough stuff. I think it was good for them to see that they could stand up for things and be heard, and they can inspire thousands of people to join them in that," she says. She then adds, "it was pretty amazing for me to see these quiet girls, cos they are super quiet, you know, they were [the type of] quiet where they would colour their faces if they laughed or smiled, you know, the modesty – the 'buckiness' is what we call it – was huge within them. If I asked them to stand up in a room, they couldn't really do that. They were super shy." Now Jasilyn is one of the key figures in the native youth movement, fighting at the forefront against pipelines such as Keystone XL and Dakota Access. And recalling a time when these now strong young people were shy adolescents, Tammy remarks that watching them today makes her proud: "to see them standing on podiums and to see them screaming their beliefs is amazing for me. I love, like, that's crazy for me to remember them, and to see them now like that, it's beautiful."

Jasilyn, Jasilea and Joseph: what they have managed to achieve is no easy task for a child or teenager. To be able to pull oneself out of a society handicapped by a heavy history of trauma; to deal with the inevitable, inescapable and omnipresent depression, suicides, poverty, crime and self-medication; and – amid all that – to make one's own path in life is proof of vitality, a desire for survival, in which CRYP has a pivotal role. Examples like these, Tammy says, make her hope "that we are able to find the way to use that and inspire and show the rest of our kids" that life is a possibility.

It is not an easy task and there are many challenges. "Kids grow up too fast here, you know," Julie says, but at CRYP things run a little differently: the clock slows down, life regains its normalcy: "they can just come here and be a kid, you know. Which is a really important part of growing up. You should be just allowed to just play and laugh and be carefree and not worry if your siblings are eating supper or if they are dressed, and that happens just far too often."

The world in which they are growing up is already cruel. Having been born with a blood tie to their land, their inheritance, is in itself a blessing and a curse. Placing a heavy burden on their shoulders, it makes them the targets of racist acts and cruelty. "What's the word? Segregate? Is that the right word? Where different kids go to different schools? Every now and then that'll come up, but kids don't want that. That's grown-ups just being stupid, you know," Julie reflects. "The kids are fine. Kids are always fine, it's what we grown-ups give them. Like it's a big gift or something, and it's not. It's the biggest anchor that we could give a child, is to give them that gift of racism or hatred," she says, "that's what we do, and it weighs them down, and pulls them down, and sometimes they can't cut loose, and they are stuck in it. So, it's a pretty ... it's a big job." And a huge challenge, considering what organisations such as CRYP are up against: "You know, we don't make the laws about how things go; we don't have that sort of impact. Tribal Government has the impact. You know, and all these bigger, bigger people, more powerful, more knowing people, know, do, you know, make a lot of the decisions that we have to kind of live with."

And at Standing Rock, for the first time in many years for some, and, for others, for the first time in their lives, it was the people themselves who were making the decisions. The camps provided an opportunity for communal decision-making, and the people, especially the youth, thrived in them.

"We don't have a hierarchy system," LaDonna says, referring to the camps at Standing Rock, "we don't have a leadership system. That is why the camps worked." She continues: "As long as you follow the traditional setting, political, spiritual, craftsmen people, the grandmas, you have a society that functions. Without, 'Hey, I'm the great emperor' or 'Hey, I'm the great ruler' or 'Everybody listen to me'. Because we are taught no man can really tell another man what to do." With a mischievous note in her voice, she adds, "so, if we all follow Trump, wouldn't we be in trouble?"

The movement that was triggered by the events at Standing Rock – all that was happening and continues to happen with Dakota Access – has touched many people on many different levels. But personal experiences were not the only thing to come out of it all. LaDonna believes that spiritual experiences – faith – also played an integral role in the Standing Rock movement. Civil disobedience through silent prayer was the motto in camps such as Sacred Stone. When referring to their form of resistance against DAPL, she feels it is necessary to stress a few points. "So, let's clarify things," she asserts:

> Sacred Stone was separate from everything else. Why? Because, in June, I looked around and watched people at the camp, and I thought, 'Wow, this is how people are supposed to live with the earth. And how do we take this and teach young people? So we applied for *501 c3*[26] to become a total green village. We separated ourselves from the demonstrations, the protests, etc.

LaDonna trusts in the healing power of prayer. She believes their form of resistance – non-violent direct action, as the protesters liked to call it – was the preferred approach in most camps at Standing Rock, coupled with a lifestyle that was the least disruptive to nature, with people staying in traditional homes as well as mobile shelters such as yurts and tipis. It helped bring order to things. "Everybody at mine had to go to prayer in the morning, prayer in the afternoon, prayer in the evening," she says, "because we were there to pray for the water. And, any given day, we had people from all over the world bringing in water to put in the river and for prayer ceremony. So, I needed us to stay like that."

Over time, people from all over the world started joining the movement, bringing their beliefs and prayers to Sacred Stone as well as to other camps. LaDonna recalls: "I said, anybody who comes stands with me, stands with me, I don't care if you are blue, purple or orange, I don't care how you pray or what you pray to, you come stand with me, you are welcome. And I stayed like that. And with that I've been so honoured to be a part of so many cultures." She also believes that a few prophecies came to pass as a result of this gathering: "So, the first prophecy is when the Seventh Generation stands up to heal the hoop. That was all the young people, who first ran to Omaha, then to Washington, DC, all the young people," she recounts, "yes, then, when the eagle and condor meet, the world would heal. So, when South America and North America came together, and that has been our prophecy. Cos the condor is a sacred bird in the South, the eagle is our sacred bird. And they have come together to stand together." And, last but not least, "when the black snake comes to devour the earth, we stand up, cos if we do not, the world would end. So, we only just begun to fight."

LaDonna tells us her dreams for the future, which she hopes to realise through the non-profit they have set up. "Our first stand for now is organic farming, so we are trying to put in as much produce as we can," she explains. They're also organising workforce training for them and, through the networking that naturally occurred at the camps, "trying to get people from Sacred Stone into all of these areas".

This in and of itself is a major undertaking, and something that excites rather than intimidates her. What she has created is now far greater than what she'd initially had in mind: "So, right now, we have Sacred Stone Louisiana, Pennsylvania, all over," she says, adding, "in Great Britain, they set up camps, the Samis have set up camps, so, to me, it's a change of mind-thought. And as we have a crazy man in the presidency, we need to stand up now." And standing up can come in different forms: LaDonna repeats that she believes in education, in training, and mentions sending her people to conferences to encourage both.

Enthusiastically, she continues to talk about their future plans: "By this fall, when we have the land situated, we can start physically building a green village. And so, for us, nothing changed. We are still out there, we are still standing up against Dakota Access, cos Dakota Access is just one pipeline, but that is not that much of our issue. Who built this?" A valid question, as is its follow-up: "Who gave it the green light?"

"I'm not quite sure which American President was our friend. Wait. None," LaDonna then laughs heartily, before adding:

It's the same thing, we are dealing with the same thing, and so, as we move forward, we got to move forward with grace, non-violent resistance, prayer and ceremony, and develop partnerships and fellowships across the world, That's where we are at. We have only just begun. And to break a movement you have to send in somebody, to cause division, gossip, rumours, yellow journalism. I didn't even know there was a word like yellow journalism, I learned about it when they said, 'Oh, there is oil in the pipe': they are not even done building! Or, 'This movement has ended', but then nobody talked to us. So, they have no idea, we move forward, we are continuing to move forward, amazing allies, amazing people, amazing partnerships from across the world. We are just now trying to save the world. And save our water. Because water should be the first and foremost of everybody's lives. Because without water, we all die. No two ways about it. Without water, we die. And so, in order to save the water, we have been saving the world, and I think it is the only reason why native people are still alive, because they have done everything to exterminate us – [but] we are still here.

Epilogue

Just as LaDonna said, in the months following the dismantlement of the camps at Standing Rock, several new ones started springing up all over the United States. With the confidence that their voices would now be heard, if not by mainstream media then definitely via social media, people who were inspired by Standing Rock, as well as those who participated directly, started new movements, large and small, or continued old ones with renewed vigour. Soon several individual movements to protect the earth and protest against exploitative "big money" mega-projects began popping up across the country.

Resistance to Dakota Access would continue in court, but there was still work that could be done on the ground with regard to other ongoing pipeline projects such as Keystone XL. Those, like Jasilyn Charger, who had fervently fought the pipeline's construction in person, and had even won a temporary victory by stopping it dead in its tracks, would take the struggle back up. With President Trump at the helm in the White House, it seemed the fight to protect the environment, the water and the interests of the Seventh Generation – which meant life itself – would not end any time soon. And when Keystone XL sprung a leak in November 2017, spilling "an estimated 210,000 gallons of oil in north-eastern South Dakota," this proved to be more pertinent than ever.[1]

Since Trump's inauguration, several pipeline projects – both new and old – have been given the green light, and as early as February 2017 separate resistance camps started cropping up in places such as Lancaster County, Pennsylvania, in protest of the Atlantic Sunrise natural gas pipeline; in Sweetwater, New Jersey, in protest of the Pilgrim Pipeline; and in the Big Bend region of Texas against the Trans-Pecos Pipeline. And, with the Federal Government clearing the path for the dumping of nuclear waste at Yucca Mountain, the former site of nuclear bomb tests above ground in the 1950s and below ground up until 1992, residents in Nevada, having suffered from bouts of cancer that they link to these tests, are now preparing to take action to reverse the decision.

Back at Standing Rock, when we arrive at the Prairie Knights Casino, we are met with a welcome surprise: the venue will be hosting a two-day seminar. The programme reads: *The Fourth Annual Fulfilling the Prophecy of the Grandfathers: Protecting the Environment through Sovereignty, Protecting our Reserved Water Rights.* There is a sizable crowd in the spacious conference room, where panellists are already taking the stage to give their presentations on subjects such as "Oil spills in the Bakken", "Gauging climate change in Indian country" and "Efforts of the water protectors of Oceti Sakowin Camp".

DAPL is by now finished and operational. On 7 June 2017, President Trump announced its opening at a speech in Cincinnati, a part of the spending spree on infrastructure he promised during his campaign:

> I'm pleased to announce that the Dakota Access Pipeline, which I just mentioned, is now officially open for business, a $3.8 billion investment in American infrastructure that was stalled and

nobody thought any politician would have the guts to approve that final leg. And I just closed my eyes and said, "Do it."[2]

He continued by saying that he didn't think it was fair for a corporation to have done all that work and be stuck at the last leg, with only a small portion of the project left to be completed. Now that it was up and running, he said, it was beautiful and "everybody is happy, the sun is still shining, the water is clean. But you know, when I approved it, I thought I would take a lot of heat, and I took none. Actually none. People respected that I approved it." Words that confirm we are living in a post-truth era.

On the legal front, there have been small victories for the water protectors, but – as is the way with justice – an ultimate one will take some time. On 14 June, a week after the President of United States boasted of his efforts in helping DAPL become operational, headlines in the United States lit up with the announcement that a federal judge in Washington had called for further environmental impact analyses into DAPL. The decision, which carried the signature of US District Judge James E. Boasberg, did not call for the pipeline to be shut down, however; instead, it advocated further study of the potential threat the pipeline posed to tribes' fishing and hunting rights. To use the exact words of Judge Boasberg, whose lengthy court decision meticulously answered requests from both the Standing Rock and Cheyenne River Sioux Tribes as well as USACE:

Although the Corps substantially complied with NEPA in many areas, the Court agrees that it did not adequately consider the impacts of an oil spill on fishing rights, hunting rights, or environmental justice, or the degree to which the pipeline's effects are likely to be highly controversial.

To remedy those violations, the Corps will have to reconsider those sections of its environmental analysis upon remand by the Court. Whether Dakota Access must cease pipeline operations during that remand presents a separate question of the appropriate remedy, which will be the subject of further briefing.[3]

So far, the district court, although sympathising with the tribes' arguments against USACE's declaration that the pipeline does not have a substantial impact on the human environment, has not found their case adequate in terms of submitted evidence – at least not adequate enough to warrant a full shutdown of the pipeline. However, with a detailed environmental review of the pipeline and its impact, to be submitted by the Corps, still pending, the possibility of a full shutdown has not been completely ruled out either. So, if both tribes can formulate a better case file and submit convincing references to prior rulings on similar cases, or further factual evidence as opposed to mere arguments, the door that Judge Boasberg leaves ajar in his ninety-one-page decision may be pushed open. And that seems to be what scares Energy Transfer Partners the most.

An environmental case highlighting human rights violations as complex as these calls for some strong and highly experienced legal counsel, and that, in the United States, is a costly endeavour: one that corporations do not flinch at and can put aside a budget for at a moment's notice, while the grassroots movements scramble to pool together their funds. And corporations such as Energy Transfer Partners know that well. When all intimidation tactics fail, and the fight is finally taken to the courts, companies do not shy away from doing all in their power to wear down their opponents. So, as the court case between the tribes and USACE continues, the energy conglomerate is now suing the environmental NGOs who took part in the Standing Rock movement for damages inflicted during their construction of the pipeline. The accusations in their lawsuit against the climate activists range from ecoterrorism to breaking the Racketeer Influenced and Corrupt Organizations Act, or RICO, a federal law that is often invoked to put members of the mafia on trial for organised crime.

What stands out in this recent lawsuit against the climate activists is the law firm representing Energy Transfer Partners: Kasowitz, Benson & Torres LLP, whose founding and managing partner, Marc Kasowitz, is President Trump's long-time lawyer. Annie Leonard of Greenpeace, in a September broadcast, said that the lawsuit brought against them is, in fact, a "SLAPP" suit, the acronym standing for "Strategic Lawsuit Against Public Participation".[4] Considering the trials against Standing Rock activists are still ongoing, despite social media campaigns demanding that the charges against them be dropped, Leonard's claim that this lawsuit "is an attempt to criminalize and silence protest, at the exact time that this country needs people rising up more than ever"[5] makes a lot of sense.

Last but not least, around the same time as the deadline for this book, and during the 28 September elections for Tribal Council at Standing Rock, former chairman David Archambault II, the very person who complied with the state-issued eviction notice for the camps, and who, by LaDonna's account, tore down Sacred Stone without giving its residents enough time to recover their belongings, succumbed to defeat. Although still heralded by some as the person who championed the Standing Rock cause, bringing the case for tribal sovereignty before the parliament in Washington and the United Nations in New York, he has now been replaced by Mike Faith, former vice chairman of the Tribal Council. Faith, having won 63% of the votes, has assumed the role of chairman for the Standing Rock Sioux Tribe. Posing for a photo opp by the side of a pickup truck, with stickers on its window displaying the words *Cowboy Up* above and *In God We Trust* below the image of an American flag imprinted on a rodeo horse and rider, Faith's effect on the future of the case still pending in court remains to be seen.[6]

Once again, this book is as much about Standing Rock and why it matters as it is an exploration of hundreds of years of history. If we were to overlook those stories from the past – if we were to view Standing Rock as an isolated environmental movement – we wouldn't be seeing the big picture. There are so many issues that are outside the scope of this book, but which are nevertheless important milestones along the path of injustice native societies have been forced to tread in the Americas, specifically the United States. From blood quantum to citizenship, from having tribal rights to being forced to sign them over in treaties, from segregation to assimilation: subjects so deep that each needs to have its own story told separately. There are many documents in the archives that tell portions of these stories, a treasure trove of data for any researcher or journalist. That said, Standing Rock is a victory, although at first sight it may not look like it. It is the latest show of resistance in a timeline full of such moments, the repercussions of which – like those of its predecessors – will transcend through time. With its individual stories of righteous disobedience and courageous solidarity still resonating, it will continue to inspire similar movements well into the future.

We are all inhabitants of this planet, and movements such as Standing Rock may be our last chance to save it. We need to realise that our tall buildings, our wide asphalt roads, our large airports and our big dams are not going to protect us from what is to come. Instead, their mere presence and continued construction will further aggravate environmental degradation.

During the last months of writing this book, within the space of a couple of weeks, at least two hurricanes made landfall in the United States, devastating the human habitat that lay in their path and calling for major evacuations. Both hurricanes were expected to be mere tropical storms; however, due to added moisture from the ocean – a direct result of global warming – they gained in intensity, upping their force to a category four. Around the same time, what would normally be seasonal rainfall in Istanbul, Turkey, turned into an unprecedented hail storm, with pieces of ice as big as golf balls coming down on the city, on unsuspecting citizens, breaking windows and destroying cars. While this natural phenomenon with its unforeseen intensity only lasted for a short while, when the ominous clouds cleared the devastation was apparent. Meanwhile, the coasts of Italy, whose major source of income is tourism, are becoming increasingly infested with a certain type of poisonous jellyfish which in the absence of any natural predators, keep multiplying in record numbers. Scientists believe that, again, global warming creating more temperate seas has provided this species, which has made its way to the Mediterranean through the most recent man-made enlargement of the Suez Canal, with a safe and comfortable breeding ground.

And on a final note, our planet has become detectably warmer, with global surface temperatures in the first half of 2017 rising 0.94 degrees Celsius above the 1950–80 average.[7]

So, in light of all this, Standing Rock stands out as an exceptional story, one in which the people of the United States, even former members of its army, chose to stand with the native population in their struggle to maintain control over their land against a large corporation, powerful politics and rampant racism, in order to protect something as basic as water.

This movement also came at a peculiar junction in the history of the United States. With Donald Trump as president, unusual governance is colouring the country's domestic and foreign policy. The racist overtones of Trump's presidential campaign have already done irrecoverable damage, polarising the nation. Now the cameras have turned away from Standing Rock. The prairie where all this happened is once again overgrown with grass, including in the parts where pipes have been stubbornly laid underground. However, its story – which at its peak was covered by news outlets of all sizes, primarily due to the unexpected gathering of tribes it inspired and the victory (albeit one that was quickly overturned by the Federal Government) for the Lakota it fuelled – is not over yet. What started at Standing Rock will continue on the next battleground, wherever that may be, with Corporate America on the one side and the tribes and their supporters on the other.

Author's Note

Native American history, as with all oral histories, is a challenging area for journalists to conduct research in. By professional definition, we are pushed to bend over backwards to tell all sides of a story based on hard fact. However, when one side's experiences have been meticulously documented and survived, while the other side's memories have largely gone missing, it is near impossible to get down to the origins of a story and reconstruct reality. That ominous Winston Churchill quote – "History is written by the victors" – perpetually breathes down our necks.

So, on that day in the Prairie Knights Casino at Fort Yates, when I told LaDonna that I couldn't find a written reference to the Black Snake Prophecy anywhere, she said, smiling, that it was because there was none: "because it must stay oral. Because we put it in writing, then it becomes a lie, because American language is up for interpretation; you can't even remember what your bible said originally. You fight over the interpretations. So, when you put it into written word, it becomes a lie."

Therefore, dear reader, this book you have read is in fact a book of lies.

When I started following the events at Standing Rock in early 2016, it was out of mere interest. Back in my own country, in Turkey, we had gone through a similar set of events and had recorded a bitter loss three years prior. The park that young people had set out to save was still there, true, but the country had changed to its core, and seemingly for the worst. Human rights abuses had amassed, while destruction everywhere else in the country was rampant and quite obvious. The park with its linden trees was still standing but everywhere else was ablaze. So, when Standing Rock happened, I secretly wished that it would succeed. And, much like everybody else, I was only looking at the surface of things.

Each major happening has its roots in history. It was true for the Gezi Park protests in Istanbul, and throughout my research for this book, it did not come as a surprise that it also held true for Standing Rock. The more I dug into the archives, the more multifaceted the story became: land grabs, assimilation, invasion, discrimination. Standing Rock had once again parted the curtain that often hangs over the United States as "the land of the free", and almost immediately everything that is often preached about the country – freedom, equality, justice – began to crumble.

When your country's foundations are corrupt, and when your government sits on colossal human rights abuses while acting as a flagship for humanitarianism, then you know there is a problem. Having covered wars and conflicts, and having specialised in forced migration for twenty-odd years, I saw within myself the right to write about Standing Rock. I am not Native American and have never lived on a reservation, but sometimes an outsider looking in, with a cool head, a candid curiosity and diverse experience, can better analyse events – keeping them at a distance and trying to stay objective.

This book is a piece of journalism about the undercurrents of Standing Rock. And, through it, I hope the series of events that unfolded during the course of 2016 at a once obscure reservation in the Great Plains, with its heroes and heroines, comes into perspective. For they are events that, coming from the past, still resonate today.

Notes

PROLOGUE

1 *Wasichu*: Lakota/Dakota for nonindigenous/white people.

2 Native Americans were not granted US citizenship until 1924.

3 "Kill the Indian, and Save the Man": famous motto of Captain Richard H. Pratt, founder of the Carlisle Indian Industrial School in Pennsylvania.

4 Generational trauma or, more accurately, transgenerational trauma is trauma that is transferred from one generation of trauma survivors to the next, often manifesting in post-traumatic stress disorders.

5 Denig, E.T. (1930). *Indian Tribes of the Upper Missouri*. Forty-sixth Annual Report of the Bureau of American Ethnology to the Secretary of the Smithsonian Institution, 1928-1929. Government Printing Office, Washington, pp. 375-628 (see p. 398).

6 White, B.M. (1994). Encounters with spirits: Ojibwa and Dakota theories about the French and their merchandise. *Ethnohistory* 41(3), 369-405.

BEFORE WE BEGIN...

1 See https://350.org/science/#warming.

2 See www.whitehouse.gov/the-press-office/2015/01/20/remarks-president -state-union-address-january-20-2015.

3 *Ibid.*

4 See https://youtube/a4PVrmLImo4.

5 See www.macleans.ca/politics/ottawa/why-david-suzuki-called-justin
-trudeau-a-twerp/.

6 See www.motherjones.com/environment/2015/10/justin-trudeau-canada
-climate-change-keystone-pipeline.

7 See http://time.com/4102868/president-obama-rejects-keystone-xl
-pipeline/.

8 www.whitehouse.gov/the-press-office/2016/01/12/remarks-president
-barack-obama-%E2%80%93-prepared-delivery-state-union-address.

9 See https://climate.nasa.gov/evidence/.

10 See www.investopedia.com/articles/insights/072416/phillips-66-vs
-conocophillips-how-they-differ-cop-psx.asp.

11 See https://online.wsj.com/public/resources/documents/TrumpFinancial
Disclosure20150722.pdf (pp. 37, 42 and 44).

12 See https://assets.documentcloud.org/documents/2838696/Trump-2016
-Financial-Disclosure.pdf (p. 37).

13 See http://docquery.fec.gov/cgi-bin/fecimg/?201607159020646897.

14 See www.usace.army.mil/Media/News-Releases/News-Release-Article
-View/Article/1003593/statement-regarding-the-dakota-access
-pipeline/.

15 See www.facebook.com/JustinPJTrudeau/videos/10155150280905649/.

16 See www.theguardian.com/environment/2017/jun/02/european-leaders
-vow-to-keep-fighting-global-warming-despite-us-withdrawal.

17 See http://earthjustice.org/sites/default/files/files/DAPL-order.pdf.

ONE

1 See www.theguardian.com/commentisfree/2016/nov/02/dakota-pipeline
-protest-bundy-militia.

2 A yurt is a portable round tent, often covered with animal skin, and used
by the Turkic and Mongolian nomads.

3 The 1804 westward bound expedition of Meriwether Lewis and William Clark into the newly acquired lands through the Louisiana Purchase of 1803, commissioned by Thomas Jefferson and carried out with
aid from the military. The group would come to be known as Corps of
Discovery, and the trail which they took would be called by the names
of the two frontiersmen leading the expedition.

4 Basso, K.H. (1996). *Wisdom Sits in Places: Landscape and Language
Among the Western Apache.* University of Mexico Press, Albuquerque,
NM.

5 See the *Encyclopedia Britannica* entry at https://global.britannica.com/
topic/Comanche-people.

6 Rosen, P. (1895). *Pa-Ha-Sa-Pah, Black Hills of South Dakota.* Nixon
-Jones Printing Co, St Louis, MO.

7 Schlesier, K.H. (1994). *Plains Indians, A.D. 500-1500: The Archaeological Past of Historic Groups.* University of Oklahoma Press, Norman, OK.

8 *Ibid.*

9 Neihardt, J.G. (2014). *Black Elk Speaks: The Complete Edition. University of Nebraska Press,* Lincoln, NE.

10 Sundstrom, L. (1996). Mirror of heaven: cross-cultural transference of the
sacred geography of the Black Hills. *World Archaeology* 28(2), 177-189.

11 *Ibid.*

12 Schlesier (1994); Sundstrom (1996).

13 Rosen (1895).

14 *Ibid.* Rosen goes on to suggest that a branch of Toltecs may have broken
off during their big migration south, and this band may have chosen
to settle around the Black Hills area: "Most probably the Crows, as a
branch of the Toltec family in their southward migration, left the main
group and crossed the Rocky Mountains about the year 1200 A.D.,
and gradually extended their meanderings as far east as the Missouri".

Thus, he tells us, the Crow *Story of Creation* is also attributable to the Black Hills, with events centring on the hill now known as Bear Butte.

15 Schlesier (1994).

16 Koestler-Grack, R.A. (2005). *Mount Rushmore*. ABDO Publishing Company, Minneapolis, MN.

17 See www.bloomberg.com/research/stocks/private/snapshot.asp?privc apId=24932174.

18 Charmaine White Face (Zumila Wobaga) (2015). Crow Butte uranium mine in Crawford, NB. Online Newsletter, October 1, Defenders of the Black Hills. URL: www.defendblackhills.org/index .php?option=com_content&view=article&id=333:meeting -october-1st-2015&catid=1:latest&Itemid=33.

19 Lupus is an auto-immune disease.

20 See www.epa.gov/uic/epa-dewey-burdock-class-iii-and-class-v-injection -well-draft-area-permits.

21 Hyde, G.E. (1993). *A Sioux Chronicle*. University of Oklahoma Press, Norman, OK.

22 *Ibid.*

23 Meeting notes of the Committee on Public Lands convened at the House of Representatives on July 13, 1949 to discuss and vote on H.R. 5372 (www.scribd.com/document/357641731/H-R-5372-Transcript -1949-07-13-pdf-213533-pdf). The proposed bill would pass as an Act at the 81st Congress on September 30, 1950 (www.loc.gov/law/help/ statutes-at-large/81st-congress/session-2/c81s2ch1120.pdf).

24 *Ibid.*

25 *Ibid.*

26 What Doug is talking about is the General Allotment Act, or Dawes Act, which passed in Congress in 1887. This culminated in the Sioux Bill and the subsequent land commission in 1889, which broke up the Great Sioux Reservation into smaller, separate reservation areas,

while putting the rest of the land up for sale to homesteaders. The Dawes Act was implemented, unsurprisingly, without consulting the tribes.

27 Lawson, M.L. (1994). *Dammed Indians, The Pick–Sloan Plan and the Missouri River Sioux, 1944–1980.* University of Oklahoma Press, Norman, OK.

28 Schneiders, R.K. (1997). Flooding the Missouri Valley: the politics of dam site selection and design. *Great Plains Quarterly*, Summer, 237–249.

29 *Ibid.*

30 *Ibid.*

31 *Ibid.*

32 See www.nps.gov/mnrr/learn/historyculture/pick-sloan-plan-part-two-debate-and-compromise.htm.

33 See www.usace.army.mil/Dakota-Access-Pipeline/.

34 See http://daplpipelinefacts.com/.

35 US Army Corps of Engineers (2015). Dakota Access Pipeline draft environmental assessment. USACE, Omaha District.

36 *Ibid.*

37 See http://bismarcktribune.com/news/state-and-regional/pipeline-route-plan-first-called-for-crossing-north-of-bismarck/article_64d053e4-8a1a-5198-a1dd-498d386c933c.html.

38 See http://abcnews.go.com/US/previously-proposed-route-dakota-access-pipeline-rejected/story?id=43274356.

39 See www.psc.nd.gov/database/documents/14-0842/001-020.pdf.

40 See www.psc.nd.gov/public/newsroom/2016/10-27-16Statementon DakotaAccessRouteConsiderations.pdf.

41 See www.youtube.com/watch?v=ZlwdtnZXmtY&t=2320s.

42 See www.usace.army.mil/Media/News-Releases/News-Release-Article-View/Article/1003593/statement-regarding-the-dakota-access-pipeline/.

43 See www.wsj.com/articles/dakota-pipelines-builder-says-obstacles-will -disappear-under-donald-trump-1479327104.

44 See http://bismarcktribune.com/news/state-and-regional/audio-tribe -objected-to-pipeline-nearly-years-before-lawsuit/article_51f94b8b -1284-5da9-92ec-7638347fe066.html?utm_medium=social&utm _source=email&utm_campaign=user-share.

45 *Ibid.*

46 In the sound recording, Standing Rock Sioux Tribe's chairman David Archambault II asserts that his tribe still recognises the 1951 and 1968 Fort Laramie Treaty Boundaries of the Greater Sioux Reservation, "which encompasses North Dakota, Wyoming, Montana, South Dakota" and includes the route for DAPL. Archambault also reminds the Energy Partners and DAPL officials of a 2012 resolution his tribe passed "that opposes any pipeline within that Treaty Boundaries, just so you know, coming in, this is something that the tribe is supporting, this is not something that the tribe does not wish." He adds that even though the territory the DAPL official was referring to is outside of the "1889 federal boundaries, we still recognise our treaty boundaries".

47 NHPA: National Historic Preservation Act.

48 NEPA: National Environmental Policy Act.

49 Nationwide Permit 12 (NWP12) applies to "activities required for the construction, maintenance, repair, and removal of utility lines and associated facilities in waters of the United States," whereas "a 'utility line' is defined as any pipe or pipeline for the transportation of any gaseous, liquid, liquescent, or slurry substance, for any purpose, and any cable, line, or wire for the transmission for any purpose of electrical energy, telephone, and telegraph messages, and radio and television communication."

50 See www.theguardian.com/commentisfree/2016/nov/02/dakota-pipeline -protest-bundy-militia.

51 See http://america.aljazeera.com/articles/2014/7/15/epa-finalizes-paint cleanupplan.html.

52 See www.nj.com/news/index.ssf/2015/04/time_to_tell_the_truth_about _the_ramapough_people.html?hootPostID=489b61fcae66ce4532 765d8b919fe0d6.

53 *Ibid.*

54 See http://toxiclegacy.northjersey.com/.

55 *Ibid.*, p. 2 of *Overview.*

56 See www.change.org/p/save-ringwood-state-park-don-t-let-ford-motor -company-use-it-as-a-toxic-landfill.

TWO

1 See www.pbs.org/warrior/content/timeline/opendoor/roleOfChief.html. NAGPRA stands for The Native American Graves Protection and Repatriation Act, which "was enacted on November 16, 1990, to address the rights of lineal descendants, Indian tribes, and Native Hawaiian organizations to Native American cultural items, including human remains, funerary objects, sacred objects, and objects of cultural patrimony. The Act assigned implementation responsibilities to the Secretary of the Interior." See also www.nps.gov/nagpra/.

2 *Mitakuye Oyasin*: "All my relations".

3 See www.facebook.com/sonsandbros/photos/a.636216583082259 .1073741828. 635774026459848/1212890448748200/?type=3.

4 The Sioux Bill passed on 2 March 1889 and carried its full purpose in its title: *An Act to Divide a Portion of the Reservation of the Sioux Nation of Indians in Dakota into Separate Reservations and to Secure the Relinquishment of the Indian Title to the Remainder, and for Other Purposes.*

5 Hyde (1993).

6 See www.lakotayouth.org/about/.

7   US Census Bureau (2016). 2015 poverty and median household income estimates – counties, states, and national. Small Area Income and Poverty Estimates (SAIPE) Program, December 2016, US Census Bureau.

8   According to CDC's Suicide Data Sheet, published in 2015, the rates of adults aged eighteen or older having suicidal thoughts in the previous twelve months were 2.9% among blacks, 3.3% among Asians, 3.6% among Hispanics, 4.1% among whites, 4.6% among Native Hawaiians/ Other Pacific Islanders, 4.8% among American Indians/Alaska Natives, and 7.9% among adults reporting two or more races. See www.cdc .gov/violenceprevention/pdf/suicide-datasheet-a.pdf.

9   IHS is Indian Health Services.

10 US Senate (2005). Oversight hearing on the concerns of teen suicide among American Indian Youths. Hearing before the Committee on Indian Affairs, 15 June, 109th Congress, Session 1. US Government Printing Office, Washington, DC. See www.gpo.gov/fdsys/pkg/ CHRG-109shrg21891/html/CHRG-109shrg21891.htm.

11 See www.nationalgeographic.com/magazine/2012/08/pine-ridge/.

12 Captain Richard Henry Pratt, founder and superintendent of the Carlisle Indian Industrial School in Pennsylvania.

13 Hyde (1993).

14 *Ibid.*

15 Captain Richard Henry Pratt (Carlisle Indian Industrial School).

16 Hyde (1993).

17 *Ibid.*

18 *Ibid.*

19 Standing Bear, L. (1978). *Land of the Spotted Eagle.* University of Nebraska Press, Lincoln, NE.

20 *Ibid.*

21 Hyde (1993).

22 Standing Bear (1978).

23 The American Indian Religious Freedom Act (AIRFA) is a US Federal Law and joint resolution of the 95th Congress (Public Law 95-341).

24 See www.ourdocuments.gov/doc.php?flash=false&doc=50&page=tr anscript.

25 Hyde (1993).

26 *Ibid.*

27 Meriam, L. (Technical Director, Institute for Government Research) (1928). *The Problem of Indian Administration.* The Johns Hopkins Press, Baltimore, MD.

28 *Ibid.*

29 Gallagher, C.A., and Lippard, C.D. (2014). *Race and Racism in the United States [4 Volumes]: An Encyclopedia of the American Mosaic.* Greenwood, Santa Barbara, CA.

30 Jacobsen-Bia, K. (2014). Radmilla's voice: music genre, blood quantum, and belonging on the Navajo nation. *Cultural Anthropology* 29(2), 385–410.

31 *Ibid.*

32 Garroutte, E.M. (2003). *Real Indians: Identity and the Survival of Native America.* University of California Press, Berkeley, CA.

33 The Onondaga Nation is an arm of the Haudenosaunee, or the Iroquois Confederacy, whose homeland is in the current State of New York (www.onondaganation.org/aboutus/facts/).

34 Garroutte (2003).

35 *Ibid.*

36 Bombay, A., Matheson, K., and Anisman, H. (2014). The intergenerational effects of Indian Residential Schools: implications for the concept of historical trauma. *Transcultural Psychiatry* 5(3), 320–338.

37 *Ibid.*

38 *Ibid.*

39 *Ibid.*

40 *Ibid.*

41 Denig (1930), p. 522.

THREE

1 See www.lakotaperspectives.com/Sitting_Bull_s_Way_of_Life.html.

2 Wishart, D.J. (1994). *An Unspeakable Sadness: The Dispossession of the Nebraska Indians.* University of Nebraska Press, Lincoln, NE.

3 Denig, E.T. (1953). *Of the Crow Nation.* Smithsonian Anthropological Papers No. 33, Bureau of American Ethnology Bulletin No. 151, Smithsonian Institution, Washington DC.

4 Wishart (1994).

5 *Ibid.*

6 The great migration of the Ojibwa (Ojibwe or Ojibway, originally the Anishinabe) is recorded extensively in the oral tradition of Ojibwa folklore. It mentions a great flood forcing the large tribe to move westward, in turn pushing off all other tribes on their path. For some of the Ojibwa myths and folklore, see Banai, E.B. (2010). *The Mishomis Book.* University of Minnesota Press, Minneapolis, MN.

7 Wishart (1994).

8 *Ibid.*; the quote at the end is from Moulton, G. E. (ed) (1987). *The Journals of the Lewis and Clark Expedition, Volume 3: August 25, 1804–April 6, 1805.* University of Nebraska Press, Lincoln, NE.

9 Kohl, J.K. (1860). *Kitchi-Gami: Wanderings Round Lake Superior.* Chapman and Hall, London.

10 Williams, R. (1643). *A Key into the Language of America.* Gregory Dexter, London.

11 Rosen, D.A. (2007). *American Indians and State Law: Sovereignty, Race, Citizenship, 1790–1880.* University of Nebraska Press, Lincoln, NE.

12 Library of Congress (1787). An ordinance for the government of the territory of the United States, north-west of the river Ohio (www.loc.gov/item/90898154/).

13 Rosen (2007).

14 *Ibid.*

15 Schlesier (1994).

16 Written as both Gardener and Gardiner, we will be using the former, as this appears in the published manuscript.

17 Gardener, L. (1660; printed 1901). *Relation of the Pequot Warres*, Chattin Carlton, W. N. (ed). The Acorn Club of Connecticut, p. xi.

18 *Ibid.*

19 *Ibid.*, p. x.

20 *Ibid.*

21 *Ibid.*, p. 17.

22 *Ibid.*, p. 21.

23 Rogin, M.P. (1991). *Fathers and Children: Andrew Jackson and the Subjugation of the American Indian.* Transaction Publishers, Piscataway, NJ, p. 4.

24 *Ibid.*, p. 130.

25 Zinn, H. (2003). *A People's History of the United States.* Harper & Row; HarperCollins, New York.

26 *Ibid.*, p. 126.

27 Rogin (1991).

28 *Ibid.*

29 "Trail of Tears" refers to a number of forced migrations of Eastern American Tribes – on foot, at times shackled, and without any provisions – west of the Mississippi as a result of the Indian Removal Act of 1830. During these journeys, several thousand tribesmen and women, including children and the elderly, perished, and the survivors were left deeply traumatised.

30 Zinn (2003), p. 126.

31 *Ibid.*, p.127.

32 Vanderwerth, W.C. (1971). *Indian Oratory: Famous Speeches by Noted Indian Chiefs.* University of Oklahoma Press, Norman, OK.

33 *Ibid.*

34 Zinn (2003), p. 127.

35 *Ibid.*, p. 128.

36 Rogin (1991).

37 Wishart (1994).

38 Schlesier (1994).

39 *Ibid.*

40 *Ibid.*

41 Vacandard, E. (2016). *Original Narratives of Early American History: Spanish Explorers in the Southern United States 1528–1543.* Barnes & Noble, Inc, New York.

42 Wishart (1994).

43 *Ibid.*

44 See https://stlgs.org/research-2/life-death/medical-disasters/cholera-epidemic-of-1849; www.stltoday.com/news/local/metro/a-look-back-cholera-epidemic-hit-a-peak-here-in/article_f50b669f-a4c8-595b-bc6a-d3d9833ffc14.html.

45 Wishart (1994).

46 Also known as Teton or Teton Sioux: "Teton (contr. of *Titonwan*, 'dwellers on the prairie'). The western and principal division of the Dakota or Sioux, including all the bands formerly ranging west of Missouri river, and now residing on reservations in South Dakota and North Dakota." (See www.accessgenealogy.com/native/teton-sioux-tribe.htm; see also www.ndstudies.gov/gr8/content/unit-iii-waves-development-1861-1920/lesson-4-alliances-and-conflicts/topic-1-us-army-dakota-territory/section-3-fort-rice-and-lakota-sioux)

47 These are Oglala, Sichangu (Brulé), Sihasapa (Blackfoot), Miniconjou, Itazipcho (Sans Arcs), O'ohenunpa (Two Kettle), and Hunkpapa (www.accessgenealogy.com/native/teton-sioux-tribe.htm).

48 See http://aktalakota.stjo.org/site/News2?page=NewsArticle&id=8309.

49 *Ibid.*

50 See www.facebook.com/pg/Standing-Rock-Sioux-Tribe-402298239798452/about/?ref=page_internal.

51 *Hoka hey*: Lakota for "let's go" or "let's roll".

52 Neihardt (2014).

53 *New York Herald*, 7 July 1876.

54 Greene, J.A. (1994). *Lakota and Cheyenne: Indian Views of the Great Sioux War, 1876-1877*. University of Oklahoma Press, Norman, OK.

55 Greasy Grass is the native name for the Little Bighorn River.

56 *Wakan Tanka* in Lakota translates directly as the Great Mystery and is often referred to as the creator of the Sioux.

57 Greene tells us that, following the Battle of Little Bighorn, "the large body of Indians that had defeated Custer continued to fragment into smaller groups in the weeks after their victory". The Oglala chief Crazy Horse and his band headed over to Montana, to the Yellowstone territory, in search of buffalo. The Hunkpapa chief Sitting Bull took his band with him along the Missouri River, and later – as the buffalo herds became harder to come by and clashes with the army more frequent – up north and across the border into Canada. However, with wild game stocks on the decline, the army in constant pursuit, and each clash with them costing the tribesmen whatever hides or meat they managed to gather, hunting to sustain the bands would prove impossible. Instead of watching his people starve, Crazy Horse would surrender and move with his followers in the summer of 1877 to the Red Cloud Agency. Both Lakota chiefs and their followers were considered as "hostiles" by the Federal Government, their mere presence a threat to Washington's long-term plans to control the native population. Upon surrender, Crazy Horse would be put under arrest and soon killed while trying to be taken into custody in the guardhouse at Camp Robinson (see Black Elk (Neihardt 2014); Hyde 1937; Greene 1994). The Oglala leader's murder would be followed in December 1890 by the assassination of Sitting Bull at the Standing Rock Agency.

58 See www.whoisleonardpeltier.info/home/facts/shootout/; www.outsideonline.com/1835141/martyrdom-leonard-peltier.

59 The movement started in the 1890s, spurred by the Paiute prophet Wovoka's vision that, one day, the earth, with all the white men on it, would perish; the tribesmen would reunite with their dead; and the antelope and the buffalo would return to the Plains. In an oral message to his followers, he preached that to achieve this the followers of his religion would have to stay away from all evil; be truthful and stay away from the white man; conduct dances every six weeks, which would last for four consecutive days; and bathe in the river on the fifth day. Today, one of the best written records of this movement is ethnologist James Mooney's book *Ghost Dance Religion and the Sioux Outbreak of 1890*, published in 1896 by the Bureau of Ethnology. In this book, Mooney reveals that, despite the massacre at Wounded Knee, the religion continued to exist six years on.

60 House of Representatives (1891). Chief Sitting Bull. Report 3375, 6 January, 51st Congress, Session 2. (H.R. 3375).

61 DeMallie, R.J. (1982). The Lakota Ghost Dance: an ethnohistorical account. *Pacific Historical Review* 51(4), 385–405.

62 *Ibid.*

63 *Ibid.*

64 Reinhardt, A. D. (2009). *Ruling Pine Ridge: Oglala Lakota Politics from the IRA to Wounded Knee.* Texas Tech University Press, Lubbock, TX.

65 Foderaro, L. W. (1990). Richard Wilson, 55, tribal head in occupation of Wounded Knee. *New York Times*, 4 February (www.nytimes.com/1990/02/04/obituaries/richard-wilson-55-tribal-head-in-occupation-of-wounded-knee.html).

66 The massacre at Whitestone Hill, North Dakota would go down in history as another of the US Army's many lows in their campaign to control the Native American tribes. According to Hyde, the nature of the US Army's aggression against peaceful Native American bands in the 1860s was proof of their attitude towards the natives. They "regarded the

Indians as wild animals and thought nothing of killing them, " and while they had been "sent to maintain peace and keep the tribes quiet, many of the officers and more of the men were soon trying to break the dreadful monotony of garrison life by starting a little Indian excitement" (Hyde, G.E. (1937). *Red Cloud's Folk: A History of the Oglala Sioux Indians.* University of Oklahoma Press, Norman, OK). On that day in September, General Sully – having followed the Dakota's trail as the tribesmen peacefully commenced their seasonal hunt – through his advance troops communicated to the Dakota bands that they needed to surrender. The bands who had set up the hunting camp included the Yanktonais, Santees, Sissetons and Tetons along with a couple of Crow families. When the news reached Sully that the Dakota refused to surrender their chiefs to his men, he descended on the camp. Despite Chief Big Head's white flag of surrender, Sully's troops killed old men as well as women and children – 150 by official count – and took the survivors as prisoners. The troops recorded seventeen casualties. Sully and his men later burnt the camp, the hides, food and all possessions belonging to the Dakota (see www.ndstudies.gov/content/massacre-whitestone-hill).

FOUR

1 McLaughlin, M.L. (1913). *Myths and Legends of the Sioux.* See www.gutenberg.org/files/341/341-h/341-h.htm.

2 Wishart (1994).

3 See www.tigerswan.com/about-tigerswan/.

4 See https://theintercept.com/2017/05/27/leaked-documents-reveal-security-firms-counterterrorism-tactics-at-standing-rock-to-defeat-pipeline-insurgencies/.

5 See www.democracynow.org/2016/9/4/dakota_access_pipeline_company_attacks_native.

6 *Ibid.*

7 *Ibid.*

8 See www.cbc.ca/news/canada/calgary/north-dakota-access-pipeline
-violence-1.3748066.

9 *Ibid.*

10 See www.theguardian.com/film/2016/oct/10/shailene-woodley-arrested
-north-dakota-pipeline-protest.

11 See www.theguardian.com/us-news/2016/oct/25/north-dakota-oil-pipeline
-protest-arrests-journalists-filmmakers.

12 See https://theintercept.com/2016/10/25/video-police-viciously-attacked
-peaceful-protestors-at-the-dakota-access-pipeline/.

13 See http://bismarcktribune.com/news/local/crime-and-courts/dapl-cases
-closed-in-march-dismissed/article_a59ebf7e-8a52-53f0-aa64
-4f9c81ef761a.html?utm_medium=social&utm_source=facebook
&utm_campaign=user-share.

14 See http://time.com/4588272/journalist-standing-rock-border/.

15 See https://cpj.org/blog/2017/02/journalists-covering-standing-rock
-face-charges-as.php.

16 *Ibid.*

17 Standing Rock Sioux Tribe versus US Army Corps of Engineers, *COM-
PLAINT FOR DECLARATORY AND INJUNCTIVE RELIEF*. See
https://earthjustice.org/sites/default/files/files/3154%201%20Complaint
.pdf.

18 *Ibid.*

19 Standing Rock Sioux Tribe versus US Army Corps of Engineers,
*MOTION FOR PRELIMINARY INJUNCTION REQUEST FOR
EXPEDITED HEARING*. See https://assets.documentcloud.org/
documents/3460833/StandingRockSiouxvUSACE-August2016.pdf.

20 See https://earthjustice.org/cases/2016/the-dakota-access-pipeline.

21 See https://cpj.org/blog/2017/02/journalists-covering-standing-rock
-face-charges-as.php.

22 See www.theguardian.com/us-news/2016/oct/31/dakota-access-pipeline -protest-investigation-human-rights-abuses.

23 See www.ohchr.org/EN/NewsEvents/Pages/DisplayNews.aspx?News ID=21274&LangID=E.

24 *Ibid.*

25 Hyde (1993).

26 *501 c3* is a reference code applied by the Internal Revenue Service to non-profit organisations, granting them tax-exempt status within the United States. The term is at times used to refer to non-profit organisations (NGOs) as well.

EPILOGUE

1 See www.theguardian.com/us-news/2017/nov/16/keystone-pipeline -leaks-estimated-210000-gallons-oil-south-dakota.

2 See www.youtube.com/watch?v=yhosIktTsl8.

3 See http://earthjustice.org/sites/default/files/files/DAPL-order.pdf.

4 See www.democracynow.org/2017/9/1/greenpeace_indigenous_water _protectors_respond_to.

5 *Ibid.*

6 Photo reference: https://nativenewsonline.net/currents/dave-archambault -ii-defeated-chairman-standing-rock-sioux-tribe-mike-faith/.

7 See www.theguardian.com/environment/climate-consensus-97-per -cent/2017/jul/31/2017-is-so-far-the-second-hottest-year-on -record-thanks-to-global-warming.

Bibliography (and suggested reading)

Journals and articles

Bombay, A., Matheson, K., and Anisman, H. (2014). The intergenerational effects of Indian Residential Schools: implications for the concept of historical trauma. *Transcultural Psychiatry* 5(3), 320–338.

Charmaine White Face (Zumila Wobaga) (2015). Crow Butte uranium mine in Crawford, NB. Online Newsletter, 1 October, Defenders of the Black Hills (www.defendblackhills.org/index.php?option=com_content&view=article&id=333:meeting-october-1st-2015&catid=1:latest&Itemid=33).

DeMallie, R.J. (1982). The Lakota Ghost Dance: an ethnohistorical account. *Pacific Historical Review* 51(4), 385–405.

Foderaro, L.W. (1990). Richard Wilson, 55, tribal head in occupation of Wounded Knee. *New York Times*, 4 February (www.nytimes.com/1990/02/04/obituaries/richard-wilson-55-tribal-head-in-occupation-of-wounded-knee.html).

Schneiders, R.K. (1997). Flooding the Missouri Valley: the politics of dam site selection and design. *Great Plains Quarterly*, Summer, 237–249.

Sundstrom, L. (1996). Mirror of heaven: cross-cultural transference of the sacred geography of the Black Hills. *World Archaeology* 28(2), 177–189.

Thornton, T.F. (1997). Anthropological studies of Native American place naming. *American Indian Quarterly* 21(2), 209–228.

White, B.M. (1994). Encounters with spirits: Ojibwa and Dakota theories about the French and their merchandise. *Ethnohistory* 41(3), 369–405.

Manuscripts and books

Banai, E.B. (2010). *The Mishomis Book.* University of Minnesota Press, Minneapolis, MN.

Basso, K.H. (1996). *Wisdom Sits in Places: Landscape and Language Among the Western Apache.* University of Mexico Press, Albuquerque, NM.

Denig, E.T. (1930). *Indian Tribes of the Upper Missouri.* Forty-sixth Annual Report of the Bureau of American Ethnology to the Secretary of the Smithsonian Institution, 1928–1929. Government Printing Office, Washington, DC, pp. 375–628.

Denig, E.T. (1953). *Of the Crow Nation.* Smithsonian Anthropological Papers No. 33, Bureau of American Ethnology Bulletin No. 151, Smithsonian Institution, Washington, DC.

Gallagher, C.A., and Lippard, C.D. (2014). *Race and Racism in the United States [4 Volumes]: An Encyclopedia of the American Mosaic.* Greenwood, Santa Barbara, CA.

Gardener, L. (1660; printed 1901). *Relation of the Pequot Warres*, Chattin Carlton, W.N. (ed). The Acorn Club of Connecticut.

Garroutte, E.M. (2003). *Real Indians: Identity and the Survival of Native America.* University of California Press, Berkeley, CA.

Greene, J.A. (1994). *Lakota and Cheyenne: Indian Views of the Great Sioux War, 1876–1877.* University of Oklahoma Press, Norman, OK.

Hyde, G.E. (1993). *A Sioux Chronicle.* University of Oklahoma Press, Norman, OK.

Hyde, G.E. (1937). *Red Cloud's Folk: A History of the Oglala Sioux Indians.* University of Oklahoma Press, Norman, OK

Koestler-Grack, R.A. (2005). *Mount Rushmore.* ABDO Publishing Company, Minneapolis, MN.

Kohl, J.K. (1860). *Kitchi-Gami: Wanderings Round Lake Superior.* Chapman and Hall, London.

Lawson, M.L. (1994). *Dammed Indians, The Pick–Sloan Plan and the Missouri River Sioux, 1944–1980.* University of Oklahoma Press, Norman, OK.

McLaughlin, M.L. (1913). *Myths and Legends of the Sioux* (www.gutenberg .org/files/341/341-h/341-h.htm).

Meriam, L. (Technical Director, Institute for Government Research) (1928). *The Problem of Indian Administration.* The Johns Hopkins Press, Baltimore, MD.

Moulton, G.E. (ed) (1987). *The Journals of the Lewis and Clark Expedition, Volume 3: August 25, 1804–April 6, 1805.* University of Nebraska Press, Lincoln, NE.

Neihardt, J.G. (2014). *Black Elk Speaks: The Complete Edition. University of Nebraska Press,* Lincoln, NE.

Reinhardt, A.D. (2009). *Ruling Pine Ridge: Oglala Lakota Politics from the IRA to Wounded Knee.* Texas Tech University Press, Lubbock, TX.

Rogin, M.P. (1991). *Fathers and Children: Andrew Jackson and the Subjugation of the American Indian.* Transaction Publishers, Piscataway, NJ.

Rosen, D.A. (2007). *American Indians and State Law: Sovereignty, Race, Citizenship, 1790–1880.* University of Nebraska Press, Lincoln, NE.

Rosen, P. (1895). *Pa-Ha-Sa-Pah, Black Hills of South Dakota.* Nixon-Jones Printing Co, St. Louis, MO.

Schlesier, K.H. (1994). *Plains Indians, A.D. 500–1500: The Archaeological Past of Historic Groups.* University of Oklahoma Press, Norman, OK.

Standing Bear, L. (1978). *Land of the Spotted Eagle.* University of Nebraska Press, Lincoln, NE.

Vacandard, E. (2016). *Original Narratives of Early American History: Spanish Explorers in the Southern United States 1528–1543.* Barnes & Noble, Inc, New York.

Vanderwerth, W.C. (1971). *Indian Oratory: Famous Speeches by Noted Indian Chiefs.* University of Oklahoma Press, Norman, OK.

Wishart, D.J. (1994). *An Unspeakable Sadness: The Dispossession of the Nebraska Indians.* University of Nebraska Press, Lincoln, NE.

Williams, R. (1643). *A Key into the Language of America.* Gregory Dexter, London.

Zinn, H. (2003). *A People's History of the United States*. Harper & Row; HarperCollins, New York.

Statistics, commission/hearing notes and government papers:

House of Representatives (1949). A bill to authorize the negotiation, approval, and ratification of separate settlement contracts with the Sioux Indians of Cheyenne River Reservation in South Dakota and of Standing Rock Reservation in South Dakota and North Dakota for Indian lands and rights acquired by the United States for the Oahe Dam and Reservoir, Missouri River development, and for other purposes. Meeting Notes on Report H.R. 5372, July 13, The Committee on Public Lands.

House of Representatives (1891). Chief Sitting Bull. Report H.R. 3375, 6 January, 51st Congress, Session 2.

Library of Congress (1787). An ordinance for the government of the territory of the United States, north-west of the river Ohio (www.loc. gov/item/90898154/).

US Army Corps of Engineers (2015). Dakota Access Pipeline draft environmental assessment. Dakota Access Pipeline draft environmental assessment. USACE, Omaha District.

US Census Bureau (2016). 2015 poverty and median household income estimates – counties, states, and national. Small Area Income and Poverty Estimates (SAIPE) Program, December 2016, US Census Bureau.

US Senate (1889). *An Act to Divide a Portion of the Reservation of the Sioux Nation in Dakota into Separate Reservations and to Secure the Relinquishment of the Indian Title to the Remainder*. Chapter 405, 2 March, 50th Congress, Session 2. Library of Congress, Washington, DC.

US Senate (2005). Oversight hearing on the concerns of teen suicide among American Indian Youths. Hearing before the Committee on Indian Affairs, 15 June, 109th Congress, Session 1. US Government Printing Office, Washington, DC.

Index